RIGBY

On Our Way to English®

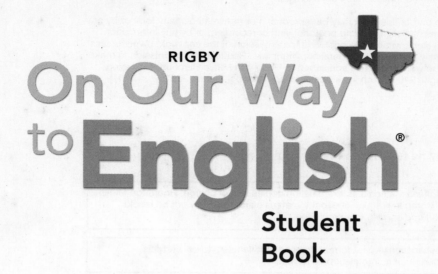

Student Book

Rigby

HOUGHTON MIFFLIN HARCOURT

Contents

My **ABC** Pages .... xiv-xv

Unit 1
School Days.............................. 2

Unit 2
Welcome to My World 34

Unit 3
Neighborhood News 66

Unit 4
Weather Wonders.................... 98

Unit 5
Animals and Their Homes 124

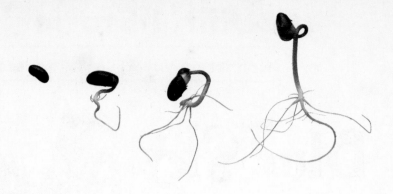

Unit 6
Away We Grow..................... 150

Unit 7
Taking Care 176

Unit 8
The Big, Beautiful Earth 202

1

Blue Sky

By Candy Rodo

2

Our School

By Luc Alexandre

Unit 2 Stories

Fiction Phonics Readers	Nonfiction Vocabulary Readers

3 — **Sam's Big Day**

By Sofia Lee
Illustrated by Pam López

4 — **Baseball!**

By Candy Rodo

5 — **Nan's Mistake**

By Cristina Moreno
Illustrated by Maria Morell

6 — **What's Cooking?**

By Lucía Casanovas

7 — **Tag**

By Roberto Gómez
Illustrated by Jordi Redondo

8 — **A Walk in the Park**

By Marcos Granados

9 — **Are You Mad, Dad?**

By Emma Riba
Illustrated by Sebastiá Martí

10 — **All Families Are Special!**

By Leslie Wong

Unit 3 Paired Stories

Fiction Phonics Readers | **Nonfiction Vocabulary Readers**

11
Packing for Camp
By Megan Linke
Illustrated by David Arnau

12
Going to Camp!
By Galila Ali

13
I Am No Rat!
By Camelia Yuen
Illustrated by Pam López

14
Animals in My Neighborhood
By Lorenzo Adams

15
Sit Still Kat!
By Megan Linke
Illustrated by Pam López

16
On the Move!
By Candy Rodo

17
Rick's Trick
By Megan Linke
Illustrated by Pam López

18
Helping in the Neighborhood
By Gladys Lalane

Unit 4 Paired Stories

19

Mack the Wild Poodle
By Megan Linke
Illustrated by Maria Morell
Part One

20

Mack the Wild Poodle
By Megan Linke
Illustrated by Maria Morell
Part Two

21

Pets and the Weather
By Sebastian Vila

22

Rain
By Candy Rodo

23

SUPERCAM
By Carla García
Illustrat...
Part One

24

SUPERCAM
By Carla García
Illustrated by David Arnau
Part Two

25

Hot or Cold?
By Candy Rodo

26

Weather Journal
By María José Ferñandez

© Houghton Mifflin Harcourt Publishing Company

Unit 5 Paired Stories

Fiction Phonics Readers   **Nonfiction Vocabulary Readers**

27

Bake Sale
By Emma Riba
Illustrated by Pam López
Part One

29

What Animals Eat
By Sebastian Vila

28

Bake Sale
By Emma Riba
Illustrated by Pam López
Part Two

30

Helpful Animals
By Marc Riba

31

Gub's New Life
By Megan Linke
Illustrat...
Part One

33

Underwater Animals
By Lionel Charles

32

Gub's New Life
By Megan Linke
Illustrated by Sebastía Martí
Part Two

34

Where Animals Live
By Candy Rodo

Unit 6 Paired Stories

Fiction Phonics Readers	**Nonfiction Vocabulary Readers**

 35

Happy Birthday

By Megan Linke
Illustrated by David Arnau

Part One

36

Happy Birthday

BOING

By Megan Linke
Illustrated by David Arnau

Part Two

 **37**

Birthdays

By Benita Masong

 **38**

When I Grow Up...

By Luz Acevedo

39

Jin's Cave

By Marvin Hampton
Illustra...

Part One

40

Jin's Cave

By Marvin Hampton
Illustrated by Jordi Redondo

Part Two

 **41**

Play Time!

By Alicia Revilla

 **42**

How Things Change

By Candy Rodo

Unit 7 Paired Stories

Fiction Phonics Readers | **Nonfiction Vocabulary Readers**

43

Peace and Quiet
Illustra

Part One

Take Care!
By Javier Gutiérrez
45

44

Peace and Quiet
By Megan Linke
Illustrated by Sebastía Martí

Part Two

46

Yams for Lunch
By M
Illustrate

Part One

Stay Safe
STOP
By Kevin Adkins
48

47

Yams for Lunch
By Megan Linke
Illustrated by David Arnau

Part Two

Unit 8 Paired Stories

Fiction Phonics Readers **Nonfiction Vocabulary Readers**

49

Pete Will Not Leave!
Illu...
Part One

50

Pete Will Not Leave!
By Emmet Tubbs
Illustrated by Pam López
Part Two

51

Our National Parks
By Kevin Adkins

52

The Be-Big Box
By ...
Illustra...
Part One

53

The Be-Big Box
By Beatriz Meléndez
Illustrated by Sebastiá Martí
Part Two

54
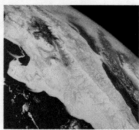
What's Big on Earth?
By Kevin Adkins

My ABC Pages

A B C D

E F G

H I J K

L M N O P

School Days

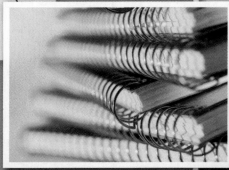

What happens in our classroom?

 Use what you know.
What do you do at school?

3

 About School!

1. What do you do in class?

write

learn

share

What did you do today?

2. Who do you see?

my teacher

my friends

Did you make new friends today?

3. What do you learn in class?

to read

to add

to ask questions

4. What do you see?

supplies

desks

windows

5. Look out the window!
What do you see there?

sky

clouds

Say **more!** Use words that describe.

Read the words. Use them.

shape

teacher

class

1. What is the shape?

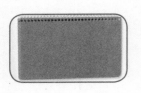  ☐  ☐

2. What is the shape?

  ☐  ☐

Talk about your class.
Talk about your teacher.

Look at the pictures. Write the words.

window

cloud

sky

1. I look out the _____.

2. I see a big, white _____.

3. I see birds in the _____.

Read the words. Use them.

write

learn

share

What do you share in class? Draw a picture.

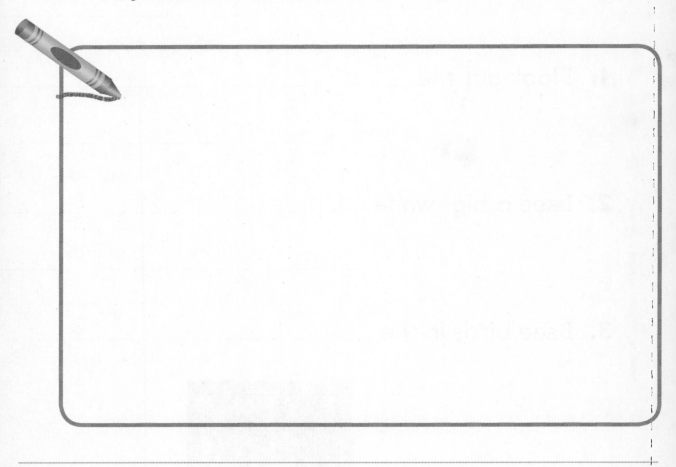

Talk About It

What can you write?
What will you learn?

Read the words. Use them.

add

ready

question

1. What do you add?

☐

☐

2. Get ready to write!
   What will you need?

☐

☐

☐

Turn and Talk

Get to know your classmate!
Ask a question.

Letters and Sounds

A. Write the letters.

B. Make a check if you hear the sound.

Sammy Seal

1.

☑

2.

☐

3.

☐

4.

☐

5.

☐

6.

☐

7.

☐

8.

☐

Letters and Sounds

A. Write the letters.

M

m

B. Make a check if you hear the sound.

Maurice Monkey

1.

☑

2.

☐

3.

☐

4.

☐

5.

☐

6.

☐

7.

☐

8.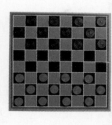

☐

Letters and Sounds

A. Write the letters.

B. Make a check if you hear the sound.

Fiona Fish

1.

☐

2.

☑

3.
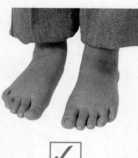
☐

4.
5
☐

5.

☐

6.

☐

7.

☐

8.

☐

Letters and Sounds

A. Write the letters.

B. Make a check if you hear the sound.

Nina Newt

1.

☐

2.

☑

3.

☐

4.

☐

5.

☐

6.

☐

7.

☐

8.

☐

Letters and Sounds

A. Write the letters.

B. Make a check if you hear the sound.

Louie Lion

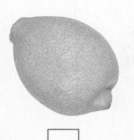

1.

☐

2.

☑

3.

☐

4.

☐

5.

☐

6.

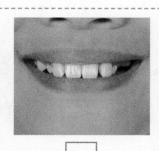

☐

7.

☐

8.

☐

Letters and Sounds

A. Write the letters.

R R

r r

B. Make a check if you hear the sound.

Ricky Raccoon

1.  ☑

2.  ☐

3.  ☐

4.  ☐

5.  ☐

6.  ☐

7.  ☐

8.  ☐

Letters and Sounds

A. Write the letters.

B. Make a check if you hear the sound.

Bonnie Bumblebee

1.

☑

2.

☐

3.

☐

4.

☐

5.

☐

6.

☐

7.

☐

8.

☐

Letters and Sounds

A. Write the letters.

K k

k k

B. Make a check if you hear the sound.

Kevin Kangaroo

1.

☐

2.

☑

3.

☐

4.

☐

5.

☐

6.

☐

7.

☐

8.

☐

Letters and Sounds

A. Write the letters.

D D

d d

B. Make a check if you hear the sound.

Daisy Dog

1.

☑

2.

☐

3.

☐

4.

☐

5.

☐

6.

☐

7.

☐

8.

☐

Letters and Sounds

A. Write the letters.

B. Make a check if you hear the sound.

Pablo Penguin

1.

☑

2.

☐

3.

☐

4.

☐

5.

☐

6.

☐

7.

☐

8.
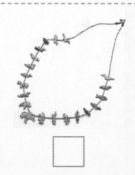

☐

Letters and Sounds

A. Write the letters.

T

t

B. Make a check if you hear the sound.

Teresa Turtle

1.

☑

2.

☐

3.

☐

4.

☐

5.

☐

6.

☐

7.

☐

8.

☐

Letters and Sounds

A. Write the letters.

H h⃗

h h⃗

B. Make a check if you hear the sound.

Hannah Horse

1.
✓

2.
☐

3.
☐

4.
☐

5.
☐

6.
☐

7.
☐

8.
☐

Letters and Sounds

A. Write the letters.

J J

j j

B. Make a check if you hear the sound.

Jill Jellyfish

1.

☐

2.

☑

3.

☐

4.

☐

5.

☐

6.

☐

7.

☐

8.

☐

Letters and Sounds

A. Write the letters.

B. Make a check if you hear the sounds.

Queen

1.  ✓	2.  ☐

3.  ☐	4.  ☐	5.  ☐
6.  ☐	7. **?** ☐	8.  ☐

Letters and Sounds

A. Write the letters.

B. Make a check if you hear the sound.

Cameron Camel

1.

☑

2.

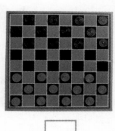

☐

3.

☐

4.

☐

5.

☐

6.

☐

7.

☐

8.

☐

Letters and Sounds

A. Write the letters.

B. Make a check if you hear the sound.

Gordon Goat

1.	2.
 ✓	 ☐

3.	4.	5.
 ☐	 ☐	 ☐
6.	7.	8.
 ☐	 ☐	 ☐

Letters and Sounds

A. Write the letters.

V ⌄

V ⌄

B. Make a check if you hear the sound.

Valentine

1.
☐

2.
☑

3.
☐

4. **5**
☐

5.
☐

6.
☐

7.
☐

8.
☐

Letters and Sounds

A. Write the letters.

W _ w_

W _ w_

B. Make a check if you hear the sound.

Wendy Walrus

1.  ✓	2.  ☐	

3.  ☐	4.  ☐	5.  ☐
6.  ☐	7.  ☐	8.  ☐

Letters and Sounds

A. Write the letters.

X x

x

B. Make a check if you hear the sounds.

Rex T-Rex

1.  ☑	**2.**  ☐

3.  ☐	**4.**  ☐	**5.**  ☐
6.  ☐	**7.**  ☐	**8.**  ☐

Letters and Sounds

A. Write the letters.

B. Make a check if you hear the sound.

Yo-yo

1.

☐

2.

☑

3.

☐

4.

☐

5.

☐

6.

☐

7.

☐

8.

☐

Letters and Sounds

A. Write the letters.

Z Z

z z

B. Make a check if you hear the sound.

Zev Zebra

1.  ☐

2. 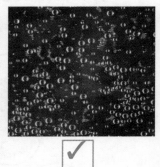 ☑

3.  ☐

4.  ☐

5. 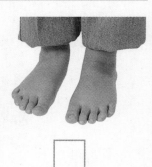 ☐

6.  ☐

7.  ☐

8.  ☐

Progress Check

Check the letter that matches.

		H ☐	T ☐	F ☐
1.	t	H ☐	T ☐	F ☐
2.	H	h ☐	b ☐	d ☐
3.	f	T ☐	F ☐	L ☐
4.	k	F ☐	D ☐	K ☐
5.	B	b ☐	k ☐	h ☐
6.	l	F ☐	T ☐	L ☐
7.	d	L ☐	D ☐	K ☐

Writing

 Listen for words you know.

Listen. Look. Write notes.

Writing

 We write left to right.

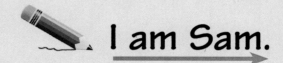 I am Sam.

 We write top to bottom.

I am Sam.
I like class.
We have fun!

Draw arrows.

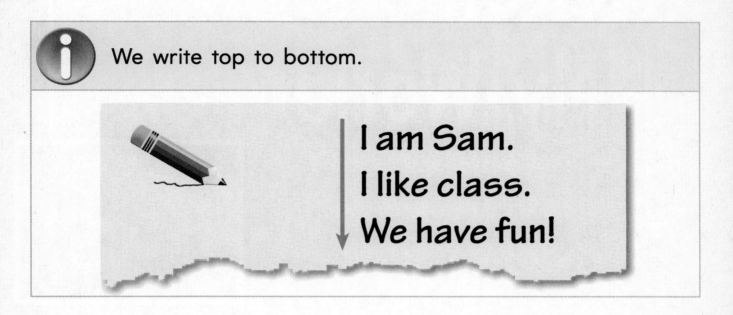

I am Mrs. Kim.

I love to teach.

I love to learn, too!

Welcome to My World

 THE BIG QUESTION How do we know about our world?

 Use your senses.

1. I use my eyes to see ____.

my dad

a fan

a map

Look around!
What do you see?

2. I hear sounds like ____!

tap, tap, tap

bam

zzzzzz

Listen!
What do you hear?

3. I can touch ____.

4. I can smell ____.

5. I can taste ____.

What is your favorite food?

How does it taste?
How does it smell?
Tell more about it.

Read the words.
Answer the questions.

hear

taste

smell

1. I can hear _____.

☐   ☐   ☐

2. I can taste and smell _____.

☐   ☐   ☐

Look at the pictures. Write the words.

family

face

special

_____

- - - - - - - - - - - - - - - - - -

1. My nose is on my _____.

_____

- - - - - - - - - - - - - - - - - -

2. I am part of a _____.

_____

- - - - - - - - - - - - - - - - - -

3. We are all _____.

Read the words. Use them.

see

use

sound

1. I use a  to make _____ .

_ _

2. I use a to _____ .

_ _

3. What do you use to eat? Draw a picture.

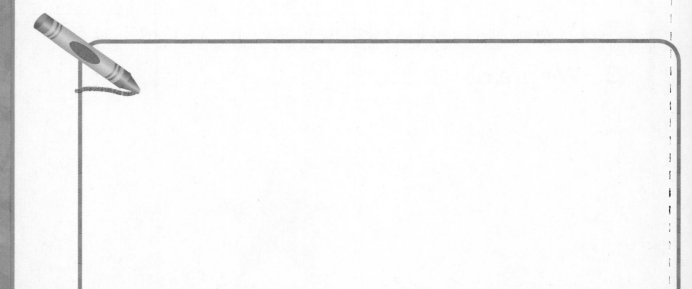

Talk about your words.

touch

senses

favorite

1. Talk about the five senses. Act them out.

2. What feels nice to touch?

3. How does your favorite teddy bear feel? Talk about it.

Letters and Sounds

A. Write the letters.

A

a

B. Make a check if you hear the sound.

Al Alligator

1.

✓

2.

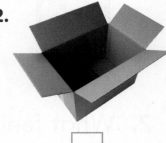

☐

3.

☐

4.

☐

5.

☐

6.

☐

7.

☐

8.

☐

Word Work

A. Read the words.

1. m   a   t   →   mat →

2. b   a   t   →   bat →

3. s   a   t   →   sat →

4. b   a   m   →   bam →

Sight Word	and
Story Word	stood

B. Listen. Spell the word.

Paired Readings

A. Write about the covers.

1.

Sam's Big Day

By Sofia Lee
Illustrated by Pam López

What do you see?

_____

- -

_____

2.

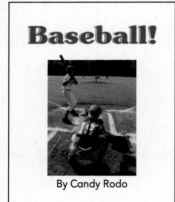

Baseball!

By Candy Rodo

What do you see?

_____

- -

_____

B. Talk about the covers.

What do you see on both?

44

Check Understanding

Sam's Big Day

1. Who is this?

☐ Tam

☐ sat

☐ Sam

2. Look. What did the fans say?

☐ Bam!

☐ Fab!

☐ Sam! Sam!

3. Show the order. Write 1, 2, or 3.

☐ ☐ ☐

Check Understanding

Baseball!

A. **Listen to the story. Complete the chart.**

1. I know this topic.	🙂	😐	😞
2. I can tell what the story is about.	🙂	😐	😞

B. **Check a box.**

1. I can hear _____.

☐   ☐

2. I can taste and smell _____.

☐   ☐

Writing

 When you write, use words that describe.

Listen. Look. Write notes.

_____
- - - - - - - - - - - - - - - - -

_____
- - - - - - - - - - - - - - - - -

_____
- - - - - - - - - - - - - - - - -

_____
- - - - - - - - - - - - - - - - -

Writing

A sentence can end in a period.
Do you see the red dot? It is called a period.

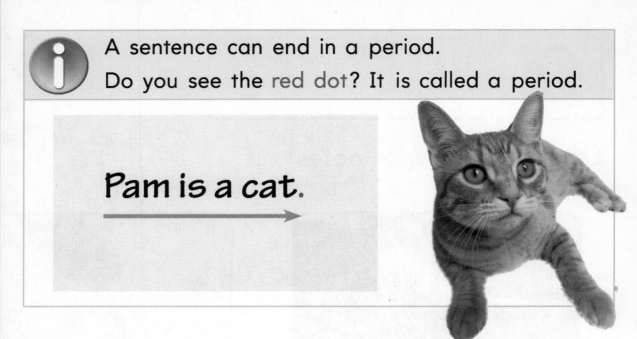

Pam is a cat.

A. Read the sentence.

Pam had a nap

B. What is missing? Fix it.

Word Work

A. Read the words.

1. f   a   n   →   fan →

2. m   a   n   →   man →

3. g   a   s   →   gas →

4. b   a   g   →   bag →

Sight Words	is me not you
Story Words	didn't why

B. Listen. Spell the word.

_____

- -

_____

Paired Readings

Look at the covers. Read the titles.

Nan's Mistake

By Cristina Moreno
Illustrated by Maria Morell

What's Cooking?

By Lucía Casanovas

Ask a **Teacher**

Talk with your teacher.
What is a *mistake*?

Turn and **Talk**

What do the titles tell you?

Check Understanding

Nan's Mistake!

1. Look at Sam.
Sam is mad.

Why is Sam mad?

"Sam is a nag." ☐

Bam! ☐

2. Look at the pot.

Why did the pot go "Bam!"?

☐

☐

Check Understanding

What's Cooking?

A. Listen to the story. Complete the chart.

1. I know this topic.	😊	😐	😞
2. I hear big ideas.	😊	😐	😞
3. I hear details.	😊	😐	😞

B. Let's pretend!
You want to bake cookies.
Circle what you will use.

 How are the stories the same?
Talk about it.

Nan's Mistake

By Cristina Moreno
Illustrated by Maria Morell

What's Cooking?

By Lucía Casanovas

Let's Count!

Listen to the sentence.
Circle the number of words.

◆
1 2 3 4 5

✖
1 2 3 4 5

1 2 3 4 5

♥
1 2 3 4 5

1 2 3 4 5

1 2 3 4 5

Letters and Sounds

A. Write the letters.

B. Make a check if you hear the sound.

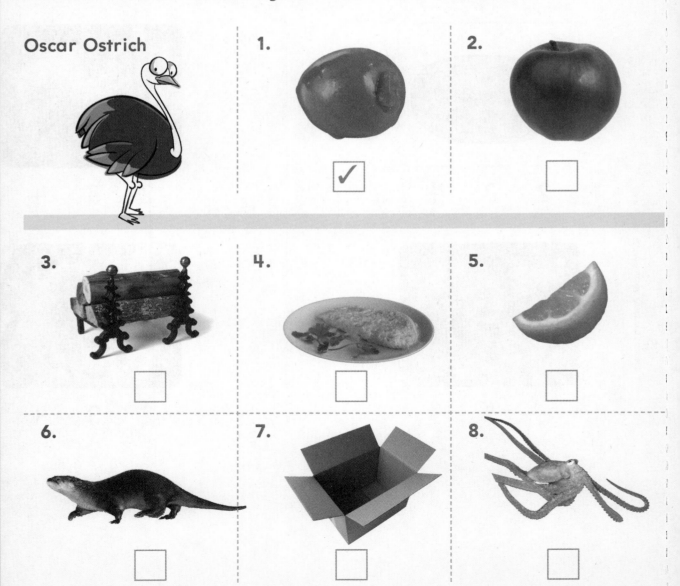

Oscar Ostrich

1. ✓

2. ☐

3. ☐

4. ☐

5. ☐

6. ☐

7. ☐

8. ☐

Word Work

A. Read the words.

1. f   o   g   fog

2. m   o   m   mom

3. s   o   b   sob

4. o   n   on

Sight Word	of
Story Word	playing

B. Listen. Spell the word.

_____

- -

_____

Word Work

 A noun names a person, place, or thing.

 The letter *s* can show more than one.

Circle the letter *s*.

3 dots	2 mats	3 bags

 What do you see?

Paired Readings

Look at the covers.

Tag

By Roberto Gómez
Illustrated by Jordi Redondo

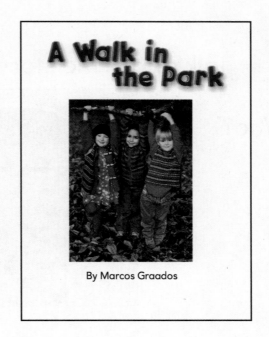

A Walk in the Park

By Marcos Graados

Turn and Talk

What will the stories be about?
Talk with a friend.

Ask a Teacher

Talk with your teacher.
What are the titles?
What do they tell you?

Check Understanding

Tag

 Talk about the story.

1. Who?

2. Where?

3. What?

Check Understanding

A Walk in the Park

A. Listen to the story. Complete the chart.

1. I know this topic.	😊	😐	😖
2. I can tell what the story is about.	😊	😐	😖

B. Answer the questions.

1. Where does the story take place?

☐   ☐   ☐

2. What do you see in the story?

☐   ☐   ☐

 Did you like the story?
Give one reason.

Word Work

A. Read the words.

1. m   a   d   mad

2. s   a   d   sad

3. d   o   g   dog

4. d   o   t   dot

Sight Words	are	did
Story Words	knew	now

B. Listen. Spell the word.

_____

- -

_____

Paired Readings

Look at the covers.

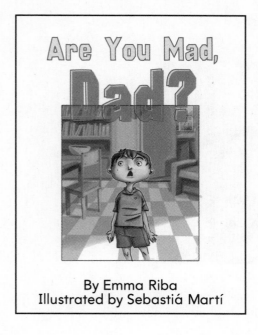

By Emma Riba
Illustrated by Sebastiá Martí

By Leslie Wong

Talk with a friend.
Describe what you see.

What are the titles?
Listen to your teacher.
Explain to a friend.

Check Understanding

Are You Mad, Dad?

1. Who asks if Dad is mad?

☐ ☐

2. Look at Dad.
What did Dad say?

☐ I am mad, Dan.

☐ Dan is mad.

☐ I am not mad.

 Look at Dan.
What is Dan doing?
Tell why.

Check Understanding

All Families Are Special!

A. Listen to the story. Complete the chart.

1. I know this topic.	☺	😐	☹
2. I can tell what the story is about.	☺	😐	☹

B. Draw what you do with your family.

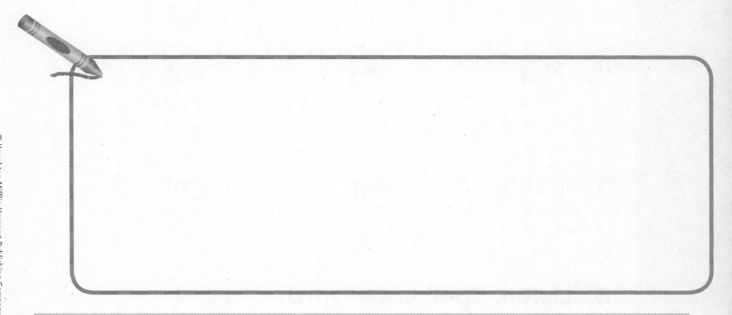

Talk About It Talk about the stories. How are they the same?

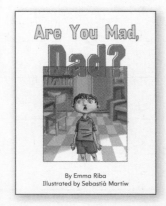

Are You Mad, Dad?

By Emma Riba
Illustrated by Sebastiá Martíw

All Families Are Special!

By Leslie Wong

Progress Check

A. Listen. Read. Check.

1. tam   □   mat   □   man   □

2. bam   □   bat   □   ban   □

3. tad   □   dad   □   dot   □

4. Nat   □   nag   □   nab   □

5. gob   □   fog   □   got   □

B. Listen. Spell each word.

1. _____

2. _____

Progress Check

Look at the picture. Check the word.

1.

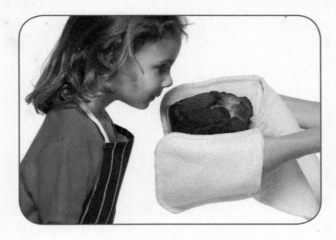

- ☐ family
- ☐ smell
- ☐ sound

2.

- ☐ see
- ☐ touch
- ☐ special

3.

- ☐ taste
- ☐ favorite
- ☐ hear

Neighborhood News

THE BIG QUESTION

How can people help their communities?

 Think about your own neighborhood. How do you help?

About the Neighborhood!

1. Let's visit _____.

the police station

the fire station

the library

my house

2. We're lost!
How do we get there?

Use a map.

Ask someone.

Look around.

3. Where do you belong?

with my family

in my neighborhood

at my school

4. What do you see in town?

a neighbor's dog

buildings and cars

a worker at work

Say **more!** Say it in a sentence.

Read the words. Write them.

town

worker

news

_____

- - - - - - - - - - - - - - - - -

1. I live in a small _____.

_____

- - - - - - - - - - - - - - - - -

2. I read the _____.

_____

- - - - - - - - - - - - - - - - -

3. An ant is a hard _____.

Talk and write about the words.

neighbor

neighborhood

belong

 Describe your neighborhood.

 Do you have a favorite neighbor?

 Where do you feel like you belong?

_____

_____

_____

Read the words. Use them.

building

locate

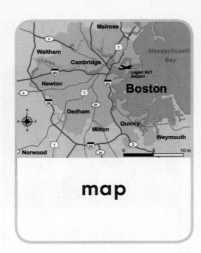

map

What building are you in now?

_____

- -

_____

Talk About It

Talk about the map.
What can you locate?

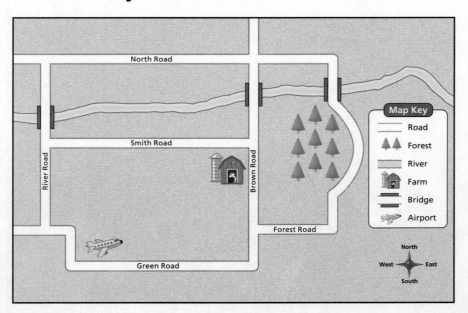

Read the words. Answer the questions.

fire station

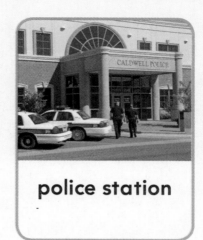
police station

library

1. What do you see at a fire station?

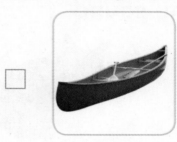

2. Who do you see at a police station?

3. What do you see at a library?

Letters and Sounds

A. Write the letters.

B. Make a check if you hear the sound.

Ingrid Iguana

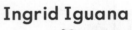

| | 1.  ✓ | 2.  ☐ |

| 3.  ☐ | 4.  ☐ | 5.  ☐ |

| 6.  ☐ | 7.  ☐ | 8.  ☐ |

Word Work

A. Read the words.

1. s   i   t   →   sit →

2. d   i   g   →   dig →

3. f   i   n   →   fin →

4. b   i   g   →   big →

Sight Words	no the what will
Story Words	bring can't know

B. Listen. Spell the word.

_____

- - - - - - - - - - - - - - - - - - - -

_____

Paired Readings

Look at the covers.

Packing for Camp

By Megan Linke
Illustrated by David Arnau

Going to Camp!

By Galila Ali

Talk with a friend.
How are the titles the same?

How are the pictures the same?
What are the people doing?

_____

- - - - - - - - - - - - - - - - - - - -

_____

- - - - - - - - - - - - - - - - - - - -

_____

Check Understanding

Packing for Camp

1. Who is Bob?

 ☐    ☐    ☐

2. Look at the bag. How big is it?

☐   Tim can fit in it.

☐   Sis can fit in it.

☐   Bob can fit in it.

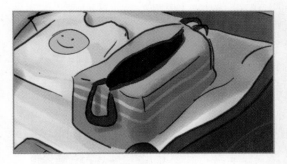

3. Show the order. Write 1, 2, or 3.

☐   ☐   ☐

Check Understanding

Going to Camp

A. Listen as your teacher reads.
Complete the chart.

1. I know this topic.	😊	😐	😦
2. I hear big ideas.	😊	😐	😦
3. I hear details.	😊	😐	😦

B. Show the order. Write 1, 2, or 3.

Writing

© Houghton Mifflin Harcourt Publishing Company

> When you take notes, use what you know.
> Tell what is happening.

Listen. Look. Write notes.

Writing

Max is a big dog.

A. Read the sentences.
Check the one that is correct.

☐ min is not big.
☐ Min is not big.

B. Write the correct sentence.

_____

- - - - - - - - - - - - - - - - - - -

_____

Word Work

A. Read the words.

1. c   a   n   can

2. c   a   t   cat

3. r   a   g   rag

4. r   i   p   rip

Sight Words	get have little stop
Story Word	arf

B. Listen. Spell the word.

Paired Readings

Look at the covers.

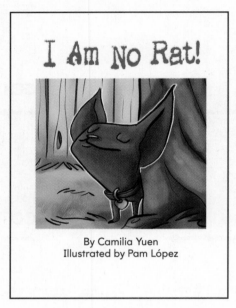

I Am No Rat!

By Camilia Yuen
Illustrated by Pam López

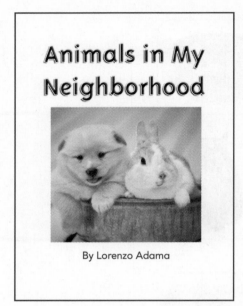

Animals in My Neighborhood

By Lorenzo Adama

Ask a Teacher

What are the titles?
Listen to your teacher.
Explain to a friend.

Turn and Talk

Talk with a friend.
What will the stories be about?

Check Understanding

I Am No Rat!

1. What is it?

☐ It is a dog.

☐ It is a cat.

☐ It is a rat.

2. Who wants to get the dog?

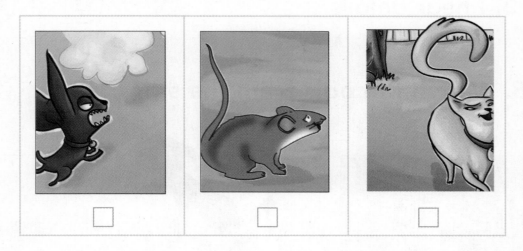

☐   ☐   ☐

3. How does Mop show he is a dog?

☐ Mop barks.

☐ Mop has a rat.

☐ Mop sat on a mat.

Check Understanding

Animals in My Neighborhood

**A. Listen as your teacher reads.
Complete the chart.**

1. I know these words.	🙂	😐	☹️
2. I hear big ideas.	🙂	😐	☹️
3. I hear details.	🙂	😐	☹️

B. Match the pals from the story.

 Did you like the story?
Give one reason.

Let's Count!

Listen. Clap the word parts.
Circle the number.

1   2   3   4   5

1   2   3   4   5

1   2   3   4   5

1   2   3   4   5

1   2   3   4   5

1   2   3   4   5

Word Work

A. Read the words.

 **1.** h   a   t   hat

 **2.** h   i   t   hit

 **3.** p   o   t   pot

 **4.** p   i   g   pig

Sight Words	last off still
Story Words	behind fell wall

B. Listen. Spell the word.

_____

- - - - - - - - - - - - - - - - - -

_____

Word Work

 An action word is a verb.
We add -s to some verbs.

I dig.

He digs.

Read the sentences.
Circle the verbs that end in -s.

1. We sit.

3. Dad naps.

2. She sits.

4. Cats nap.

Paired Readings

Look at the covers.

SIT STILL
Kat!

By Megan Linke
Illustrated by Pam López

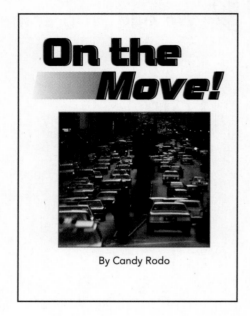

On the
Move!

By Candy Rodo

Talk about what you see.

Think about the titles.
How will the stories be the same?
Make a guess.

Check Understanding

Sit Still Hat!

1. What did the hat do first?

☐ It fell off a table.

☐ It sat still.

☐ It hit a dog.

2. What was in the hat?

☐   ☐   ☐

3. When did the hat sit still?

☐ when the dog sat still

☐ when Pat ran off

☐ when Pip the cat ran off

Check Understanding

On the Move!

A. Listen as your teacher reads.
   Complete the chart.

1. I know about this topic.	😊	😐	☹️
2. I can tell what the story is about.	😊	😐	☹️

B. Read the word from the story.
   Check the word that rhymes.

1. past	far	fast	base
	☐	☐	☐

2. race	round	up	base
	☐	☐	☐

 How are the stories the same?

By Megan Linke
Illustrated by Pam López

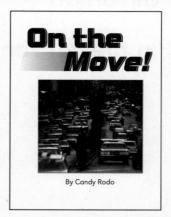

By Candy Rodo

Word Work

A. Read the words.

1. k   i   ck   →   kick →

2. k   i   d   →   kid →

3. s   o   ck   →   sock →

4. p   a   ck   →   pack →

Sight Words	my take too
Story Words	head soup

B. Listen. Spell the word.

_____

- -

_____

Paired Readings

Read the titles. Flip through the books.

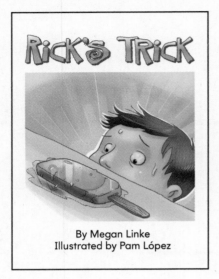

By Megan Linke
Illustrated by Pam López

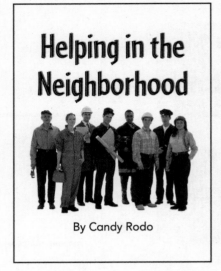

By Candy Rodo

What do you see in *Rick's Trick*?

_____

- - - - - - - - - - - - - - - - -

_____

What do you see in
Helping in the Neighborhood?

_____

- - - - - - - - - - - - - - - - -

_____

Talk About It

Where do these stories take place?

Check Understanding

Rick's Trick

1. Why did Rick hack, hack, hack?

☐ Rick is sick.

☐ Dad said, "Grab a rag!"

☐ Rick is sick of ice pops.

2. Rick said his ____ is hot.

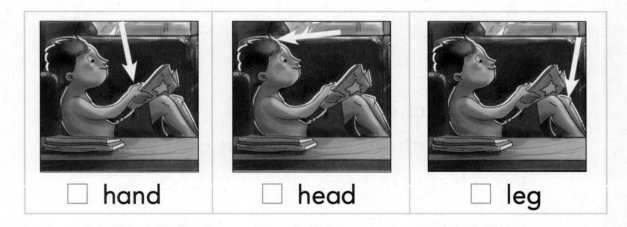

☐ hand   ☐ head   ☐ leg

3. Dad gets Rick ____.

☐ ice pops

☐ rags

☐ hot soup

Check Understanding

Helping in the Neighborhood

A. Listen as your teacher reads.
Complete the chart.

1. I know about this topic.	☺	😐	☹
2. I hear big ideas.	☺	😐	☹
3. I hear details.	☺	😐	☹

B. Make a check.
You can check more than one picture.
Who helps in the neighborhood?

☐   ☐   ☐   ☐

Progress Check

A. Show how well you are reading.

1. How is the speed?	🙂	😐	😞
2. Are the words right?	🙂	😐	😞
3. Can you hear feeling?	🙂	😐	😞

B. Fill in the chart.

Easy Words	Words to Work on

Progress Check

A. Listen. Read. Check.

1. rock   Rick   rack

□   □   □

2. hit   kit   hip

□   □   □

3. hick   hack   hag

□   □   □

4. cat   kid   kit

□   □   □

5. pit   pat   pin

□   □   □

B. Listen. Spell each word.

1. _____

2. _____

Progress Check

Match the word with the picture.

1.

- [ ] town
- [ ] worker
- [ ] neighborhood

2.

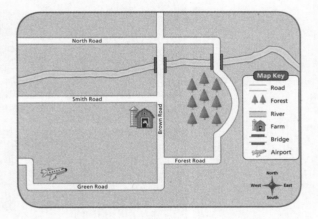

- [ ] map
- [ ] neighbor
- [ ] news

3.

- [ ] police station
- [ ] fire station
- [ ] library

Weather Wonders

 THE BIG QUESTION How does the weather affect us?

 Use what you know. Can the weather change your plans?

About the Weather!

1. What tells you about the weather?

the news   a thermometer   my eyes

2. On rainy days, I _____.

 wear rain boots

 stay inside

 get wet

Do you like rainy days?
Tell why or why not.

3. What is the weather like today?

rainy

sunny

cloudy

snowy

windy

clear

 Say **more!**   How can you tell?
What are the clues?

Read the words. Draw pictures.

rainy

Draw a rainy day.

sunny

Draw a sunny day.

weather

Draw your favorite weather.

Talk and write about your words.

cloudy

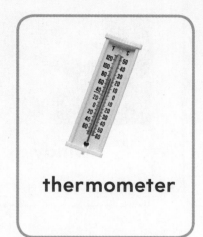

thermometer

outside

Talk with a friend.
Describe a cloudy day.

When do you use a thermometer?

Complete the sentence.
When do you play outside?

I play outside when

Look at the pictures. Write the words.

snowy

windy

wear

_____

- - - - - - - - - - - - - - - -

1. On a _____ day, I fly a .

_____

- - - - - - - - - - - - - -

2. On a _____ day, I make a .

_____

- - - - - - - - - - - - - - - -

3. On a rainy day, I _____ .

Talk and write about the words.

clear

wait

temperature

_____

- -

1. Water is _____ .

_____

- -

2. I _____ to cross the street.

_____

 Look at each picture.
What is the temperature?

Letters and Sounds

A. Write the letters.

E

e

B. Make a check if you hear the sound.

Emily Elephant

1.

✓

2.

☐

3.

☐

4.
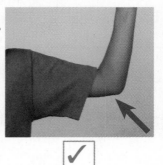
☐

5.

☐

6.

☐

7.

☐

8.

☐

Word Work

> If you see two different consonants, say both sounds.
> st = s + t

A. Read the words.

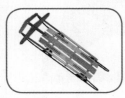

1. s   l   e   d   →   sled →

2. h   e   n   →   hen →

3. n   e   s   t   →   nest →

4. b   e   ll   →   bell →

Sight Words	for by to all
Story Words	cold wild

B. Listen. Spell the word.

_____

- -

_____

Word Work

 We combine words to make a contraction.

I am

I am ⟶ I'm

A. Circle the apostrophe.

1. I am ⟶ I'm
2. he is ⟶ he's
3. it is ⟶ it's

B. Read each sentence. Then go to .

1. I am Mack.

2. It is hot.

 Talk with a friend.
Say each sentence the short way.

Paired Readings

Look at the covers. Write about them.

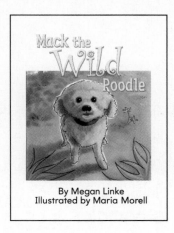

By Megan Linke
Illustrated by Maria Morell

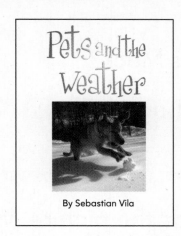

By Sebastian Vila

1. Look at *Mack the Wild Poodle*. Where is the dog?

_____

- -

_____

2. Look at *Pets and the Weather*. Where is the dog?

_____

- -

_____

Guess what the stories will be about.

Check Understanding

Mack the Wild Poodle

1. Who is Mack?

☐ a bug ☐ a dog ☐ a kid

2. Look at the picture. Where is Mack?

☐ in his house

☐ outside

☐ at school

3. When Mack gets out, what does he do?

☐ He sits on a mat.

☐ He hops and digs.

☐ He licks a bug.

Writing

A report explains or tells about something.

Look at the pictures. Write a report.

Writing

 Some action words need -s.

She hops.

A. Read the sentences.
Check the one that is correct.

☐ She kick.

☐ She kicks.

B. Write the correct sentence.

_____

- - - - - - - - - - - - - - - - -

_____

Check Understanding

Rain and *Pets and the Weather*

A. Listen as your teacher reads *Rain*.
Complete the chart.

1. I know this topic.	☺	😐	☹
2. I hear big ideas.	☺	😐	☹
3. I hear details.	☺	😐	☹

B. Show the order in *Rain*. Write 1, 2, or 3.

Talk about the stories.
How are they the same?
How are they different?

By Candy Rodo

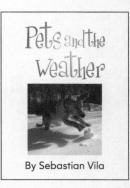

By Sebastian Vila

Letters and Sounds

 The letter *a* can stand for:

short *a*.	long *a*.

 👁 Be on the lookout.
Some short words end in *e*.
See the *e*? It makes the *a* long.

tap   tap*e*

Check the words with long *a*.

1.

   ☐   ☐   ☐

2.

   ☐   ☐   ☐

Word Work

A. Read the words.

1. 👁 c a p e → e   cape →

2. 👁 s a f e → e   safe →

3. 👁 d a t e → e   date →

4. 👁 g a m e → e   game →

Sight Words	like one this
Story Words	bird fly

_____

- - - - - - - - - - - - - - - - -

B. Listen. Spell. _____

C. Write a sentence with the word.

_____

- - - - - - - - - - - - - - - - -

_____

Word Work

 We add 's to form a possessive.

a kid's bag

Al's cape

Dad's mug

**Read the words. Ring the 's.
Then go to** .

1. a man's mop

2. Mom's bag

3. Nick's cat

4. a dog's tag

5. a kid's sock

 Talk to a friend.
Tell who owns each object.
Say it in a sentence.

Paired Readings

A. Look at the covers. Read the titles.

By Carla Gacía
Illustrated by David Arnau

By Candy Rodo

 **Ask a Teacher**

What does *Supercam* mean?
Can you think of a similar word?

B. Write about the stories.

1. Look at *Hot or Cold?* What do you see?

_____

- -

_____

2. Look at *Supercam.* What do you see?

_____

- -

_____

Check Understanding

Supercam

A. Show the order. Write 1, 2, or 3.

☐   ☐   ☐

B. Answer the questions.

1. Why did Mom get mad at Cam?

☐ Cam got a wild cat.

☐ The hat rack hit Dad.

☐ His cape hit a cup and made a mess.

2. At the end, what did Cam say?

☐ I am Cameron the Great!

☐ I am Supercam!

☐ I am a wild cat!

Put It Together!

Listen. Repeat. Say the word. Check the picture.

1. ☐ ☐ ☐

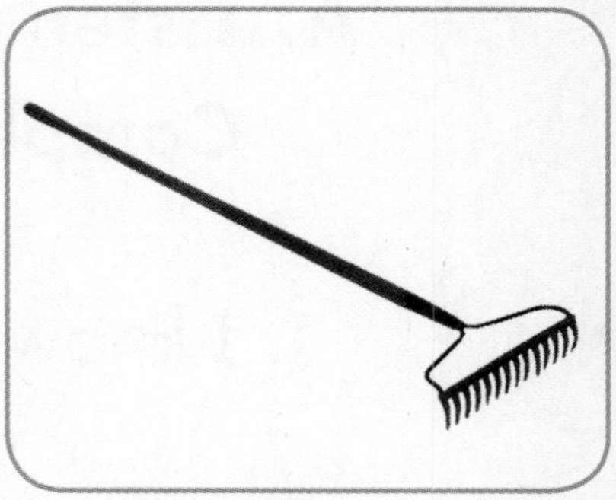

2. ☐ ☐ ☐

3. ☐ ☐ ☐

Check Understanding

Hot or Cold? and *Weather Journal*

A. Listen as your teacher reads *Hot or Cold?* Complete the chart.

1. I know these words.	😊	😐	😧
2. I can tell what the story is about.	😊	😐	😧

B. Think about *Hot or Cold?* Check the right word.

1.
      hot ☐   cold ☐

2.
      hot ☐   cold ☐

C. Talk about *Weather Journal.*

 What is the story about? Retell it to a friend.

Progress Check

A. Show how well you are reading.

1. How is the speed?	🙂	😐	😦
2. Are the words right?	🙂	😐	😦
3. Can you hear feeling?	🙂	😐	😦

B. Fill in the chart.

Easy Words	Words to Work On

Progress Check

A. Look at the underlined letters.
Check the word that has the same sound.

1. lo<u>ck</u>		
cat	log	pal
☐	☐	☐

4. pa<u>l</u>		
pat	pan	fell
☐	☐	☐

2. h<u>e</u>m		
hit	neck	ham
☐	☐	☐

5. f<u>a</u>de		
fad	came	fed
☐	☐	☐

3. ca<u>b</u>		
cap	cad	back
☐	☐	☐

6. d<u>e</u>ck		
pad	peck	kit
☐	☐	☐

B. Listen. Spell the word.

_____

1. _____

_____

2. _____

Progress Check

Look at the picture. Check the word.

1.

☐ rainy

☐ snowy

☐ sunny

2.

☐ sunny

☐ rainy

☐ cloudy

3.

☐ snowy

☐ cloudy

☐ rainy

Animals and Their Homes

 THE BIG QUESTION What makes a place feel like home?

ⓘ Use what you know. Think of your own home.

Let's Talk

About Animal Homes!

1. Where can an animal live?

in a nest   in the ground   in grass

2. What is an example of a habitat?

a forest   a pond   a desert

What makes each one special?

3. Why does an animal leave its home?

to gather food   to get water

4. Why does it return?

to rest   to feed its young   to keep warm

Say more! Say a longer sentence. Use the word *or*.

Look at the pictures.
Answer the questions.

animals

home

nest

1. Which are animals?

☐   ☐   ☐

2. What can live in a nest?

☐   ☐

Talk About It

Where do you feel at home?

Look at the pictures. Write the words.

pond

return

ground

_____

- -

1. The duck has left its _____ .

_____

- -

2. It pecks at the _____ .

_____

- -

3. Soon, it will _____ home.

Look at the pictures. Use the words.

forest

live

gather

What animals live in a forest? Draw them.

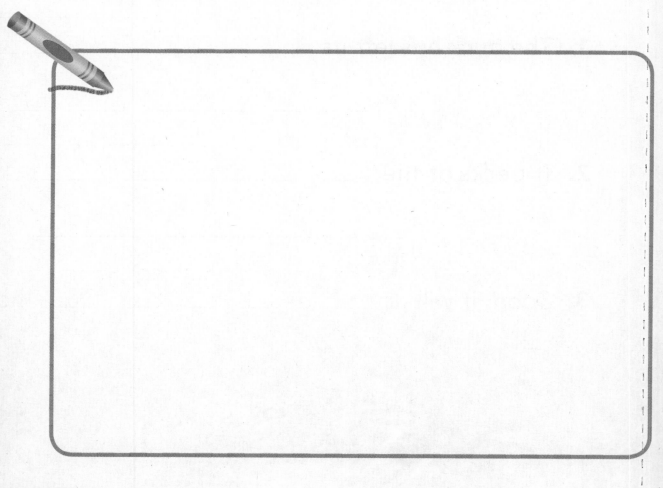

Talk About It

What do forest animals gather?

Look at the pictures. Use the words.

desert

habitat

grass

_____

- - - - - - - - - - - - - - - - -

1. A _____ is very dry.

_____

- - - - - - - - - - - - - - - - -

2. Sometimes, _____ grows in the sand.

Talk about a desert.
Describe the habitat.

Word Work

A. Read the words.

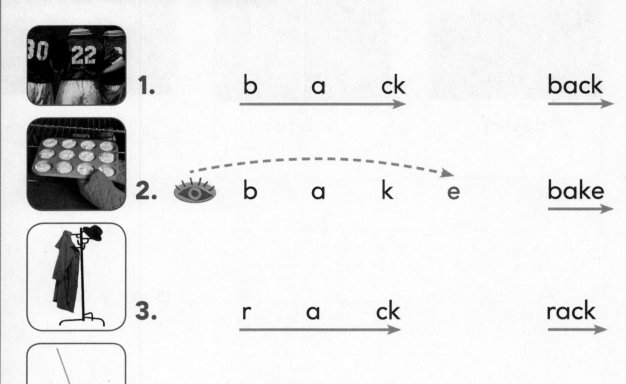

1. b a ck   →   back →

2. 👁 b a k e   bake →

3. r a ck   →   rack →

4. 👁 r a k e   rake →

Sight Word	we
Story Word	together

_____

- - - - - - - - - - - -

B. Listen. Spell. _____

C. Write a sentence with the word.

_____

- - - - - - - - - - - -

_____

132

Word Work

 A compound word is made up of two words.

cup   +   cake   =   cupcake

A. Draw a line to divide the compound word.

1. pickup

2. backpack

3. catnap

4. setback

B. Make compound words.
Use the words in the box.

| pig | hill | pen | top |

1. _____

   _ _ _ _ _ _ _ _ _ _

2. _____

   _ _ _ _ _ _ _ _ _ _

Paired Readings

Look at the covers. Flip through the books.

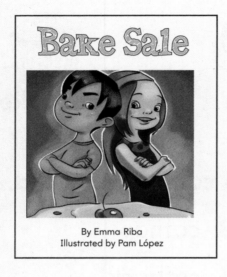

By Emma Riba
Illustrated by Pam López

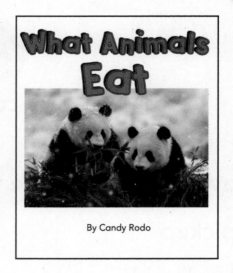

By Candy Rodo

Which story is about people?
Which story is about animals?

Make a guess. What will
the stories have in common?

Check Understanding

Bake Sale

1. Who made a cake for the bake sale?

   ☐ just Mack

   ☐ just Meg

   ☐ Mack and Meg

2. Mack says Meg's cake is ____.

   ☐ bad

   ☐ sick

   ☐ sad

3. As Mack picked up his cake, ____.

   ☐ the cake fell

   ☐ Mack ate it

   ☐ Meg ate it

Writing

Look at the pictures. Write a story.

Writing

 We can use **and** to make a longer sentence.

The fox is little.

The fox is quick.

The fox is little and quick.

A. Read the sentences.

The hog is big.

The hog is fat.

B. Use *and.* **Make a longer sentence.**

_____

- -

_____

Check Understanding

What Animals Eat and *Helpful Animals*

A. Listen to *What Animals Eat.*
Complete the chart.

1. I know these words.	😊	😐	😞
2. I can tell what the story is about.	😊	😐	😞

B. Look at both stories.
Match the animal with what it does.

1.

eats nuts ☐   eats fish ☐

2.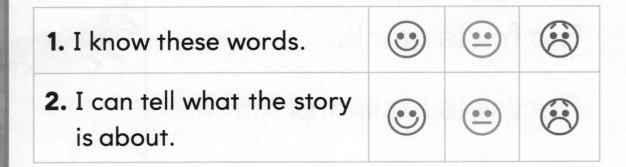

makes honey ☐   eats bugs ☐

Letters and Sounds

A. Write the letters.

B. Make a check if you hear the sound.

Umbrella

1.

☑

2.

☐

3.

☐

4.

☐

5.

☐

6.

☐

7.

☐

8.

☐

Word Work

A. Read the words.

1. d   u   ck   →   duck →

2. s   u   n   →   sun →

3. t   u   b   →   tub →

4. h   u   g   →   hug →

Sight Words	be see way where
Story Words	fish sniff

B. Listen. Spell the word.

_____

- - - - - - - - - - - - - - - - -

_____

Word Work

 We add *-s* to show more than one.

 cat    cats

A. Add *-s* if you see more than one.

1. dog _____

2. lake _____

3. nut _____

B. Circle each plural *-s*.
Then read the sentences.

1. The rats ate nuts.

2. The ducks ate bugs.

3. The bugs had lots of legs.

Paired Readings

Look at the covers. Flip through the books.

By Megan Linke
Illustrated by Sebastiá Martí

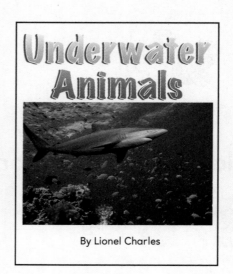

By Lionel Charles

1. Look at *Gub's New Life.* What do you see?

_____

- -

_____

2. Look at *Underwater Animals.* What do you see?

_____

- -

_____

Make a guess. How will the stories
be the same?

Check Understanding

Gub's New Life

A. Show the order. Write 1, 2, or 3.

  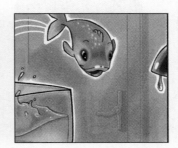

B. Answer the questions.

1. What happens after Gub sees a way up?

☐ Gub sees a duck.

☐ Gub leaves home.

☐ Gub sees mud, suds, and muck.

2. At the end, where is Gub?

☐ in a lake

☐ on the sun

☐ with Mom and Dad

Listen and Clap!

Listen. Clap the word parts.
Circle the number.

1 2 3 4 5

1 2 3 4 5

1 2 3 4 5

1 2 3 4 5

1 2 3 4 5

1 2 3 4 5

Check Understanding

Where Animals Live and Underwater Animals

A. Listen to *Where Animals Live.*
Complete the chart.

1. I know these words.	😊	😐	☹️
2. I hear big ideas.	😊	😐	☹️
3. I hear details.	😊	😐	☹️

B. Look at both stories.
Match the animal with the habitat.

1.   forest   desert   ocean
□   □   □

2.   forest   desert   ocean
□   □   □

3.   forest   desert   ocean
□   □   □

Progress Check

A. Show how well you are reading.

1. How is the speed?	🙂	😐	☹️	
2. Are the words right?	🙂	😐	☹️	
3. Can you hear feeling?	🙂	😐	☹️	

B. Fill in the chart.

Easy Words	Words to Work On

Progress Check

A. Look at the underlined letters.
   Check the word that has the same sound.

1. ma<u>k</u>e		
made	cup	mane
☐	☐	☐

4. t<u>u</u>g		
got	tag	luck
☐	☐	☐

2. tu<u>ck</u>		
tug	kid	gap
☐	☐	☐

5. <u>u</u>p		
pop	cap	hug
☐	☐	☐

3. hu<u>t</u>		
hid	hum	ten
☐	☐	☐

6. <u>g</u>un		
bag	pun	tack
☐	☐	☐

B. Listen. Spell the word.

1. _____

2. _____

Progress Check

Look at the picture. Check the word.

1.

- ☐ forest
- ☐ return
- ☐ pond

2.

- ☐ forest
- ☐ desert
- ☐ nest

3.

- ☐ gather
- ☐ desert
- ☐ pond

Progress Check

Look at the picture. Complete the sentence.

1. Peg and Sam are by a _____.

   ☐ rug

   ☐ hut

   ☐ lake

2. Peg and Sam have _____.

   ☐ pups

   ☐ rods

   ☐ cups

Away We Grow

What does it mean
to grow older?

Use what you know.
How have you changed?

Let's Talk

About Change!

1. What happens as animals grow?

   They get older.

   They get bigger.

   They change shape.

2. What happens as time goes by?

 kitten ➝  cat

 cub ➝  bear

 duckling ➝  duck

152

3. How do plants change?

A seed grows.

A bud opens.

Plants make fruit.

4. How do people change?

A baby becomes a child.

A child becomes an adult.

How are you different from how you were?

Say **more!** Say it another way.
Use the word *but*.

Look at the pictures.
Write the words.

baby

adult

child

How do we grow? Write the words in order.

1.

_____
- - - - - - - - - - - - - -
_____

2.

_____
- - - - - - - - - - - - - -
_____

3.

_____
- - - - - - - - - - - - - -
_____

154

Use your words.

kitten

cat

older

1. Draw a cat.

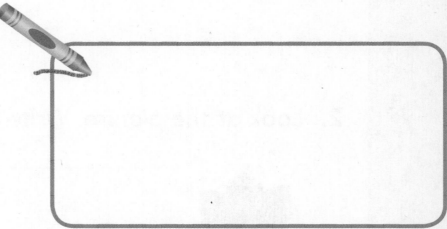

2. Draw a kitten.

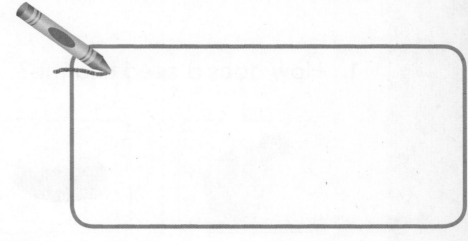

3. Which one is older?

_____

- - - - - - - - - - - - - - - - - -

_____

Read the words. Use them.

seed

change

leaf

1. How does a seed change?

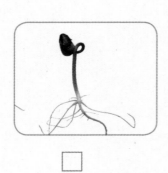

☐   ☐   ☐

2. Look at the picture. Write the word.

_____

- - - - - - - - - - - - - - -

_____

Look at the pictures. Write the words.

time

bigger

fruit

_____

- - - - - - - - - - - - - - - -

1. Change takes _____.

_____

- - - - - - - - - - - - - - - -

2. The buds will grow _____.

_____

- - - - - - - - - - - - - - - -

3. Soon, there will be _____.

Letters and Sounds

 The letter *o* can stand for:

short *o.* 	long *o.*	

  Some short words end in *e*.
See the *e*? It makes the *o* long.

mop   **mope**

 O can come at the end of a short word.
It makes the long *o* sound.

so

Find the word with long *o*.

☐   ☐   ☐

Word Work

A. Read the words.

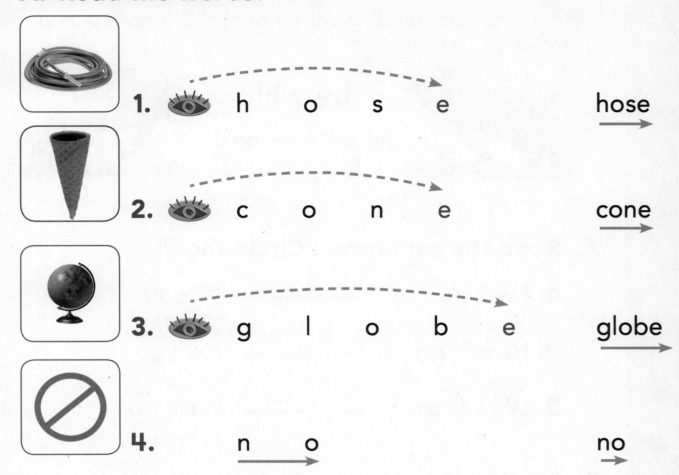

1. hose   **hose** →

2. cone   **cone** →

3. globe   **globe** →

4. n → o   **no** →

Sight Words	day don't here
Story Words	birthday happy Saturday

B. Listen. Spell the word.

_____

- - - - - - - - - - - - - - - - -

_____

Word Work

We can combine words to make a contraction.

he will

he will ⟶ he'll

A. Read the sentences. Circle the '_ll_.

1. I will go. ⟶ I'll go.

2. He will go. ⟶ He'll go.

3. We will go. ⟶ We'll go.

B. Read each sentence. Then go to .

1. He will get a home run.

2. I will make a mess.

 Say each sentence again.
Use a contraction.

Paired Readings

Look at the covers.

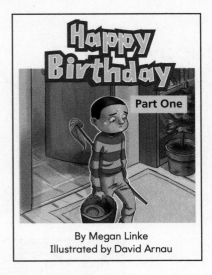

By Megan Linke
Illustrated by David Arnau

By Benita Masong

Look at *Happy Birthday*.
Does the boy look happy?
Guess why or why not.

What word do you see in both titles?

_____

- -

_____

Check Understanding

Happy Birthday

1. Nick wakes up, and he is happy. Why?
   - ☐ He is ten.
   - ☐ He has ten jokes.
   - ☐ He has a map.

2. Look at the picture. Nick has a sad face. Why?
   - ☐ It is Saturday.
   - ☐ Nick got up late.
   - ☐ No one says "Happy Birthday."

3. Mom tells Nick to clean up the deck. Why?
   - ☐ His pals are on the deck.
   - ☐ The deck is a mess.
   - ☐ Nick had a bad tone, and Dad is mad.

Writing

A report explains something.

When you write a report, use words that describe.

Look at the pictures. Write a report.

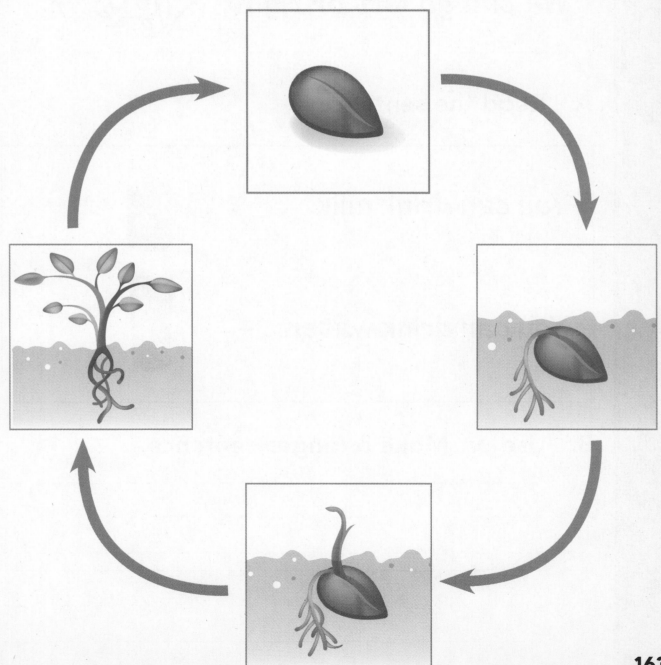

Writing

> Use *or* to join sentences.
>
> *Or* means one or the other—not both.

We can go left.
We can go right.

We can go left **or** right.

A. Read the sentences.

You can drink milk.

You can drink water.

B. Use *or*. Make a longer sentence.

_____

- - - - - - - - - - - - - - - - -

_____

_____

- - - - - - - - - - - - - - - - -

_____

Check Understanding

Birthdays and When I Grow Up...

A. Listen to *Birthdays*. Fill in the chart.

1. I know about this topic.			
2. I can tell what the story is about.			

B. Answer the questions about *Birthdays*.

1. Which is a piñata?

☐   ☐   ☐

2. Which is a cupcake?

☐   ☐   ☐

C. Talk about *When I Grow Up....*

Talk with a friend.
Sum up the story.

Word Work

A. Read the words.

1. w e t   →   **wet** →

2. v a n   →   **van** →

3. 👁 w a v e   **wave** →

4. 👁 j o k e   **joke** →

Sight Words	he yes

_____

- - - - - - - - - - - - - - - -

B. Listen. Spell. _____

C. Write a sentence using the word.

_____

- - - - - - - - - - - - - - - -

_____

166

Word Work

 We add -s to some action words. Add -s if *he*, *she*, or *it* is doing the action.

A. Circle the final -s. Then read the sentences.

1. I run.   ⟶   It runs.

2. I hum.   ⟶   He hums.

3. We sit.   ⟶   She sits.

B. Add -s to the action word. Then write it on the line.

1. I run.   ⟶   She _____.

2. I hum.   ⟶   It _____.

3. We sit.   ⟶   He _____.

Paired Readings

Look at the covers. Flip through the books.

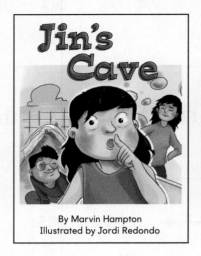

By Marvin Hampton
Illustrated by Jordi Redondo

By Alicia Revilla

1. Look at *Jin's Cave*. What do you see?

_____

- - - - - - - - - - - - - - - - - - -

_____

2. Look at *Play Time!* What do you see?

_____

- - - - - - - - - - - - - - - - - - -

_____

Make a guess. What will
the stories have in common?

Check Understanding

Jin's Cave

1. The story, *Jin's Cave*, is set ____.

   ☐ in a cave

   ☐ at Jin's home

   ☐ at a lake

2. Mom is upset when ____.

   ☐ Sun says Jin is in a cave

   ☐ Sun takes a jet

   ☐ Mom sees the cave

3. When Mom sees the "cave," she is ____.

   ☐ sad

   ☐ mad

   ☐ glad

Rhyming Words

Listen. Find the word that rhymes.

1.

   ☐   ☐   ☐

2.

   ☐   ☐   ☐

3.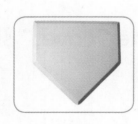

   ☐   ☐   ☐

Check Understanding

Play Time! and *How Things Change*

A. Listen to *Play Time!* Complete the chart.

1. I know about this topic.	😊	😐	😞
2. I hear big ideas.	😊	😐	😞
3. I hear details.	😊	😐	😞

B. Think about *Play Time!* What can you play alone?

☐ ☐ ☐

C. Answer questions about *How Things Change*.

1. What does a kitten become?   a dog   a cat   a kitten

☐ ☐ ☐

2. What does a seed become?   a plant   a kid   an adult

☐ ☐ ☐

Interview

 We speak differently to different people.
With teachers, speak formally.
Remember to say "Ms.," "Mrs.," or "Mr."
With friends, first names are okay.

Ask what people were like when they were little.

Ask a Friend	Ask a Teacher

 Switch roles.
Let a friend interview you.

Progress Check

A. Look at the underlined letters.
   Check the word that has the same sound.

1. g<u>o</u>		
not	note	got
☐	☐	☐

4. c<u>o</u>n		
mop	can	cone
☐	☐	☐

2. j<u>o</u>ke		
sock	so	dot
☐	☐	☐

5. <u>w</u>eb		
vet	mat	woke
☐	☐	☐

3. <u>J</u>in		
jacks	so	bin
☐	☐	☐

6. wa<u>v</u>e		
vet	gaze	off
☐	☐	☐

B. Listen. Spell each word.

1. _____

2. _____

Progress Check

Look at the picture. Check the word.

1.

   ☐ baby

   ☐ adult

   ☐ kitten

2.

   ☐ adult

   ☐ kitten

   ☐ cat

3.

   ☐ leaf

   ☐ seed

   ☐ fruit

Progress Check

Look at the picture below. Complete each sentence.

1. The dog has a ____.

bone	cone	ham
☐	☐	☐

2. On his neck, the dog has a ____.

hose	net	rope
☐	☐	☐

3. The dog has a bug on his ____.

back	nose	leg
☐	☐	☐

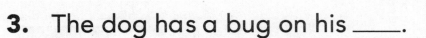

Taking Care

How can we take good care of ourselves?

Use what you know.

How do you care for yourself?

About Taking Care!

1. How do you keep healthy?

I exercise.

I eat well.

I sleep well.

I wash up!

2. What helps you stay safe?

a helmet

my seat belt

Why is it important to remember these things?

3. How else do you care for yourself?

Say more!

Make a longer sentence.
Use the word *and*.

Read the words.

Answer the questions.

clothes

meal

healthy

1. What clothes do you wear when it is hot?

☐   ☐   ☐

2. Which is a healthy meal?

☐   ☐   ☐

Look at the pictures. Write the words.

wash

exercise

sleep

_____

1. I always _____ my hands.

_____

2. I _____ to keep fit.

_____

3. I _____ at night.

Say the words. Act them out.

Read the words. Use them.

safe

seat belt

remember

_____

- - - - - - - - - - - - - - - - - - -

1. A _____ keeps me safe.

_____

- - - - - - - - - - - - - - - - - - -

2. I always _____ to wear it!

 What else keeps you safe? Write a sentence.

_____

- - - - - - - - - - - - - - - - - - -

_____

Look at the pictures. Use the words.

clean

happy

care

1. Which face is clean?

 ☐

 ☐

2. Which face is happy?

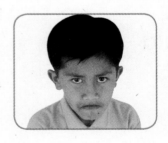 ☐

 ☐

Talk About It

Do you take care of anything? How?

Word Work

A. Read the words.

1. y   a   k   yak

2. s   i   x   six

3. b   o   x   box

4. qu   i   ck   quick

Sight Words	only would
Story Words	loud quiet

B. Listen. Spell the word.

_____

_____

_____

Word Work

 We add *-ing* to tell that something is happening now.

rain + ing ⟶ raining

A. Circle the *-ing*. Then read the sentences.

1. It is raining.

2. The kids are yelling.

B. Add *-ing* to the action words. Then read the sentences.

1. Baby Rick is cry _____ .

2. He is go _____ to bed.

Paired Readings

Look at the covers.

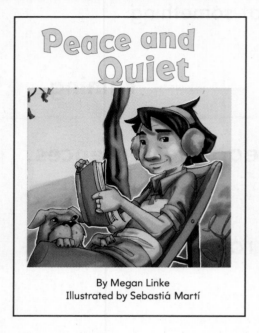

Peace and Quiet

By Megan Linke
Illustrated by Sebastiá Martí

Take Care!

By Javier Gutiérrez

Look at *Peace and Quiet*.
What is the man wearing?
Guess why.

_____

- -

_____

Talk about the titles.
What do they tell you
about the stories?

Check Understanding
Peace and Quiet

A. Show the order. Write 1, 2, or 3.

☐   ☐   ☐

B. Answer the questions.

1. Why does the man pack his bags?

☐ He has a cab.

☐ It is too noisy.

☐ He likes the noise of ducks and dogs.

2. What is it like at the lake?

☐ Ducks quack and a dog barks.

☐ It is hot at the lake.

☐ It is quiet at the lake.

Writing

Look at the pictures. Use them to write a report.

Writing

 Use **but** to put two sentences together.

José ran.

I did not.

José ran, **but** I did not.

A. Read the sentences.

Rafi likes milk.

I do not.

B. Use *but*. Make a longer sentence.

_____

- -

_____

Check Understanding

Take Care

A. Listen as your teacher reads *Take Care*.
Complete the chart.

1. I know these words.	😊	😐	😢
2. I can tell what the story is about.	😊	😐	😢

What is the story about? Sum it up.

B. What should you do every day?
Check one.

exercise   see a doctor   sneeze

☐ ☐ ☐

Letters and Sounds

 The letter *i* can stand for:

short *i*.	long *i*.

 👁 Be on the lookout.

Some short words end in *e*.

See the **e**? It makes the *i* long.

    rip   rip**e**

 Some short words end in *i* or *y*.

These words have a long *i* sound, too.

    h**i**   m**y**

Find the word with the long *i* sound.

☐   ☐   ☐

Word Work

A. Read the words.

> ℹ️ Some letters are silent.
> The letters *wr* stand for the same sound as *r*.

1. 👁 wr i t e → write

2. 👁 n i n e → nine

3. h i → hi

4. f l y → fly

Sight Word	done

B. Listen. Spell.

192

Word Work

We can add *-ly* to describing words. Then the word describes how something is done.

sad + ly ——⟶ sadly

A. Read the sentences.

1.

Carlos is sad.

2.

Carlos sadly tore it up.

3.

The cat is quick.

4.

The cat quickly ran off.

B. Circle the *-ly* ending. Then read the sentences.

1. Ride your bike safely!

2. I ate it quickly.

3. The sun shone dimly.

Paired Readings

Write and talk about the covers.

By Megan Linke
Illustrated by David Arnau

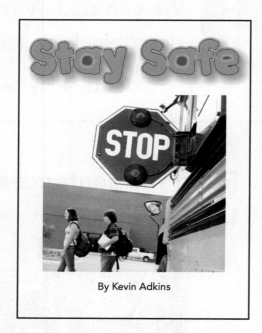

By Kevin Adkins

1. Look at *Yams for Lunch*.
What do you see?

_____

- -

_____

2. Look at *Stay Safe*. Where are the kids?

_____

- -

_____

Talk with a friend. What do you know
about staying safe?

Check Understanding

Yams for Lunch

1. How are Mick and Mike alike?

☐   Mike and Mick like to play.

☐   Mike and Mick like yams.

☐   Mike and Mick like cats.

2. What do the boys do with the yams?

☐   Mick and Mike feed the yams to the dog.

☐   Mick and Mike eat the yams. Then they go for a bike ride.

☐   Mick eats the yams. Mike feeds the yams to the dog.

3. What does Mick like? You can check more than one box.

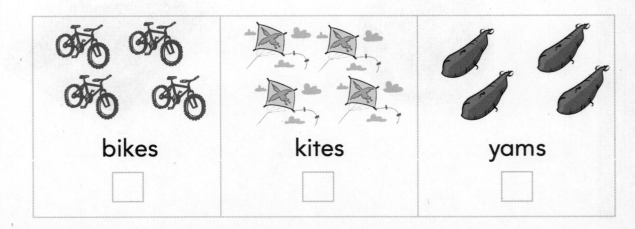

bikes	kites	yams
☐	☐	☐

Take It Apart!

Listen. Repeat the word.
Then say the sounds.

1.

2.

3.

4.

5.

6.

Check Understanding

Stay Safe

A. Listen to *Stay Safe*.
Complete the chart.

1. I know these words.	🙂	😐	☹️
2. I hear big ideas.	🙂	😐	☹️
3. I hear details.	🙂	😐	☹️

B. Check the picture that goes with the words.

1. Use a seat belt.

☐ ☐ ☐

2. Wear a helmet.

☐ ☐ ☐

Interview

 With teachers, speak formally. Remember to say, "Excuse me." With friends, you can be more relaxed.

Ask how people care for themselves.

Ask a Friend	Ask a Teacher

 Switch roles.
Let a friend interview you.

Progress Check

A. Look at the underlined letters.
Check the word that has the same sound or sounds.

1. <u>y</u>et		
in	yak	Tex
☐	☐	☐

4. sa<u>x</u>		
sack	fix	sag
☐	☐	☐

2. <u>qu</u>it		
wit	kit	quack
☐	☐	☐

5. h<u>i</u>de		
hid	time	hip
☐	☐	☐

3. <u>wr</u>ite		
nine	well	red
☐	☐	☐

6. m<u>y</u>		
size	yam	mill
☐	☐	☐

B. Listen. Spell each word.

1. _____

2. _____

Progress Check

Look at the picture. Check the word.

1.

☐ clothes

☐ meal

☐ seat belt

2.

☐ sleep

☐ exercise

☐ wash

3.

☐ happy

☐ care

☐ remember

Progress Check

Look at the picture.
Complete the sentence.
Check the word.

1. The kids all fly ____.

kits   kites   bikes

☐   ☐   ☐

2. There are ____ kites.

nine   six   five

☐   ☐   ☐

3. As the kids run, the kites ____.

rise   quit   hide

☐   ☐   ☐

The Big, Beautiful Earth

THE BIG QUESTION

Why should we protect Earth?

Use what you know.

What parts of Earth have you seen?

Let's Talk
About Our Earth!

1. Where are you now?

in my town

in my state

in my country

on our Earth

2. What parts of Earth have you seen?

mountains

oceans

rivers

What parts of Earth do you find beautiful?

3. Why do we go outside?

 to play in the sun

 to sit in the shade

 to see rocks, grass, and flowers

4. What can we do to help Earth?

 recycle

 turn off the lights

 clean up a park

What problems do these actions solve?

 Make your sentence longer.

Read the words. Use them.

mountain

ocean

Earth

1. Draw a mountain.

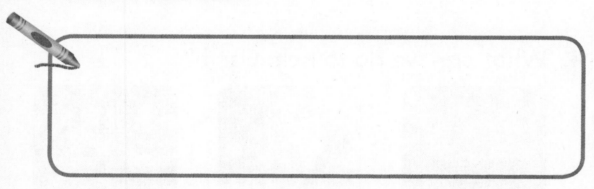

2. Draw an ocean.

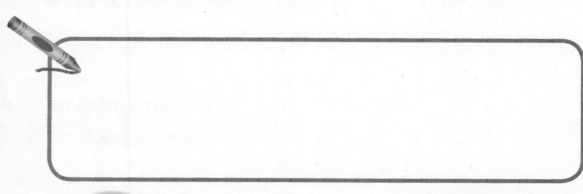

Talk About It

What do you love about Earth?

Look at the pictures. Write the words.

park

beautiful

shade

_____

1. I go to the _____ to play.

_____

2. I sit by a tree for _____.

 What is beautiful to you?
Write a sentence.

_____

_____

_____

Read the words. Use them.

country

river

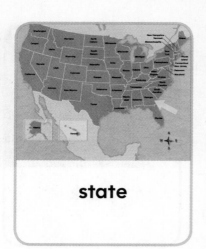

state

Draw a river.

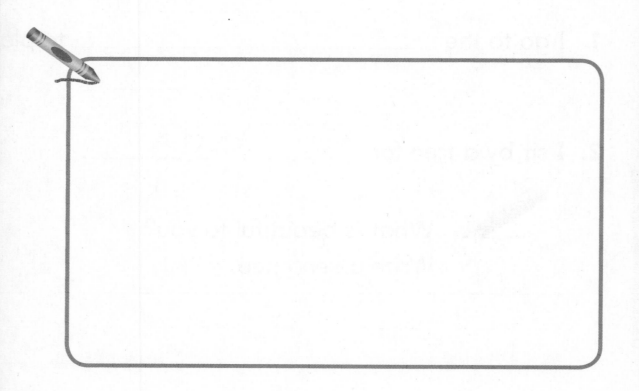

 Talk About It

Talk about your state.
Talk about your country.

Look at the pictures. Write the words.

rock

solve

save

_____

1. I see a gray _____ .

_____

2. I can _____ this problem!

_____

3. Can we _____ Earth?

Letters and Sounds

The letter *e* can stand for:

short *e*.

long *e*.

Some short words end in *e*.
These words have a long *e* sound.
The letters *ee* make the same sound.

he

bee

Remember that *e* at the end of a word sometimes changes a vowel sound.

pet   Pet*e*

Listen. Find the word with the long *e* sound.

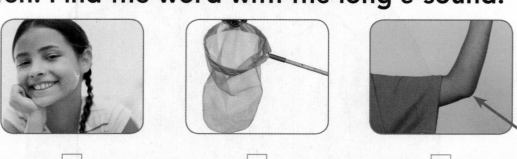

☐   ☐   ☐

Word Work

A. Read the words.

1. m   e   ss   mess

2. m   e   me

3. t   r   ee   tree

4. s   ee   d   seed

Sight Words	she why
Story Words	nurse pain

_____

- -

B. Listen. Spell. _____

C. Use the word. Write a sentence.
_____

- -

_____

Word Work

 Remember that you can put two words together to make a contraction.

I am Pete. = **I'm Pete.**

A. Read the sentences.

1.

It is red.
It's red.

2.

He is mad.
He's mad.

3.

I am sick of it.
I'm sick of it.

4.

We will hide it.
We'll hide it.

B. Make a contraction.

1. She is nice. ⟶ _____ nice.

2. We will see. ⟶ _____ see.

Paired Readings

Write about the covers.

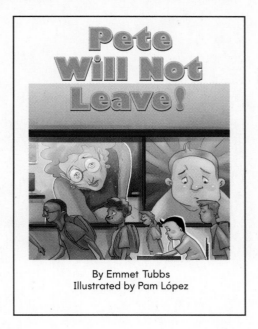

By Emmet Tubbs
Illustrated by Pam López

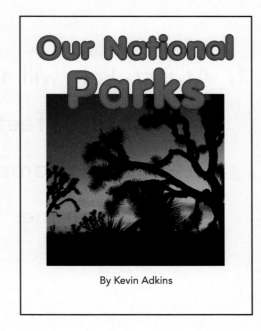

By Kevin Adkins

1. Look at *Pete Will Not Leave!*
Are the kids inside or outside?

_____

- -

_____

2. Look at *Our National Parks.*
Is the picture set inside or outside?

_____

- -

_____

Talk about the stories. Make a guess.
How will they be different?

Check Understanding

Pete Will Not Leave!

1. At first, Pete will not ____.

   ☐ get to his feet

   ☐ read his name

   ☐ tell the time

2. Pete tells Miss Alba ____.

   ☐ he has P.E.

   ☐ he feels sick

   ☐ he feels sad

3. Pete ____.

   ☐ needs a nap

   ☐ has a bad back

   ☐ has a rip

Writing

© Houghton Mifflin Harcourt Publishing Company

 When you write a story, tell what is happening. Use words that describe.

Look the pictures. Use them to write a story.

Writing

Read the sentences.

 Some words join sentences.

I see rocks **and** trees.

It is pretty, **but** it is cold.

We can hop **or** run.

A. Read the sentences.

The ocean is big.

The ocean is beautiful.

B. Join the sentences. Write a new one.

_____

- - - - - - - - - - - - - - - - -

_____

_____

- - - - - - - - - - - - - - - - -

_____

Check Understanding

Our National Parks

**A. Listen to *Our National Parks.*
Complete the chart.**

1.	I know about this topic.	☺	😐	☹
2.	I can tell what the story is about.	☺	😐	☹

B. Check the picture that goes with the words.

1. See the glow of a volcano.

☐ ☐ ☐

2. Sit in the shade of a forest.

☐ ☐ ☐

Letters and Sounds

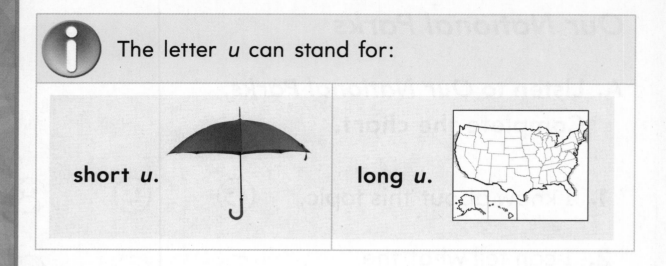

The letter *u* can stand for:

short *u*.   **long *u*.**

Some short words end in *e*.
See the *e*? It makes the *u* long.

      cut   **cut*e***

Listen. Find words with the long *u* sound.

1.

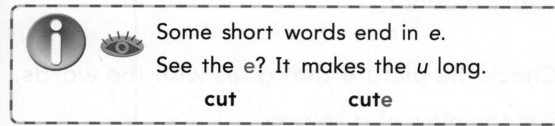

☐   ☐   ☐

2.

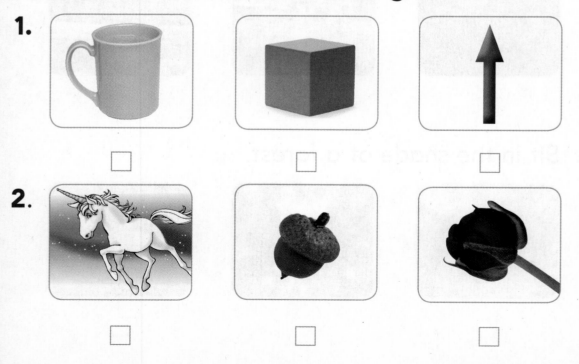

☐   ☐   ☐

Word Work

> C can stand for the sound in *cat*.
> It can also stand for the sound in: **cent**
>
> G can stand for the sound in *gas*.
> It can also stand for the sound in: **gem**

A. Read the words.

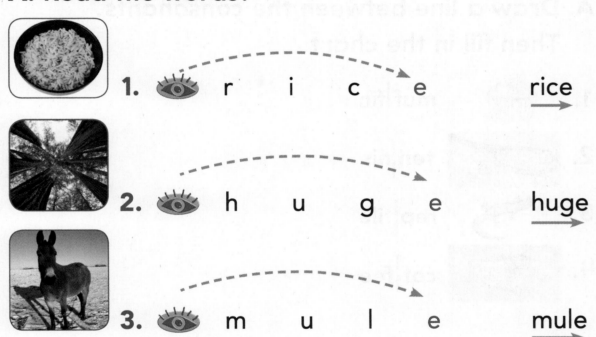

1. 👁 r i c e   rice →

2. 👁 h u g e   huge →

3. 👁 m u l e   mule →

Sight Words	do said
Story Words	grow turned

B. Listen. Spell.

Word Work

Break a long word into smaller parts.
Look for two consonants in a row.
Split the word between the consonants.

 pup|pet

A. Draw a line between the consonants.
   Then fill in the chart.

1.	 muf|fin		
2.	ten|nis		
3.	rep|tile		
4.	cof|fee		

B. Draw a line between the consonants.
   Then read the word.

1. until   4. ignore

2. mistake   5. rabbit

3. attic   6. invite

Paired Readings

Look at the covers. Read the titles.

The Be-Big Box

By Beatriz Meléndez
Illustrated by Sebastiá Martí

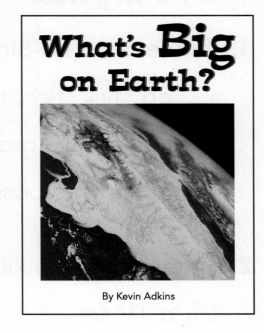

What's Big on Earth?

By Kevin Adkins

What word do you see in both titles?

_____

- -

_____

Talk About It Make a guess. What will these stories have in common?

Turn and Talk Talk with a friend. What can you name that is big on Earth?

Check Understanding

The Be-Big Box

1. In the ad, a Be-Big Box can ____.

   ☐ go "tick, tick, tick"

   ☐ make a kid grow

   ☐ make time pass

2. In ten days, the kids get ____.

   ☐ a TV set

   ☐ tubes and pipes

   ☐ a Be-Big Box

3. The Be-Big Box did not ____.

   ☐ get set up

   ☐ fit at home

   ☐ make kids big

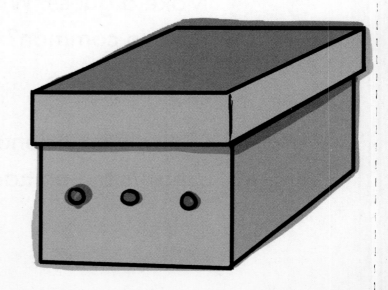

Take It Apart!

Listen. Say the word.
Then say the sounds.

1.	**4.**
2.	**5.**
3	**6.**

Check Understanding

What's Big on Earth?

A. Listen to *What's Big on Earth?*
Complete the chart.

1. I know about the topic.	☺	☺	☹
2. I hear big ideas.	☺	☺	☹
3. I hear details.	☺	☺	☹

B. Answer the questions.

1. Which country has the most people?

☐   ☐   ☐

2. Everything in this story is ____.

small   blue   big

☐   ☐   ☐

Interview

© Houghton Mifflin Harcourt Publishing Company

 We speak differently to different people. With teachers, speak formally. Remember to say, "Please" and "Thank you." With friends, you can be more relaxed.

Ask what parts of the world people have seen.

Ask a Friend	Ask a Teacher
_____	_____
- - - - - - -	- - - - - - -
_____	_____
- - - - - - -	- - - - - - -
_____	_____
_____	_____
- - - - - - -	- - - - - - -
_____	_____
- - - - - - -	- - - - - - -
_____	_____

 Switch roles.

Let a friend interview you.

Progress Check

A. Look at the underlined letters.
Check the word that has the same sound.

1. w<u>e</u>		
pet	Pete	wet
☐	☐	☐

4. mi<u>c</u>e		
mat	sit	cat
☐	☐	☐

2. m<u>ee</u>t		
Eve	met	ten
☐	☐	☐

5. ja<u>zz</u>		
zip	Jack	pass
☐	☐	☐

3. c<u>u</u>be		
cub	tune	huge
☐	☐	☐

6. tu<u>b</u>e		
fuse	rude	tub
☐	☐	☐

B. Listen. Spell each word.

_____

1. _____

_____

2. _____

Progress Check

Look at the picture. Check the word.

1.

   ☐ ocean

   ☐ river

   ☐ mountain

2.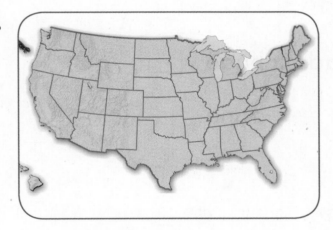

   ☐ state

   ☐ country

   ☐ park

3.

   ☐ rock

   ☐ shade

   ☐ Earth

Progress Check

Look at the picture.
Complete the sentence.

1. The baby has made a huge ____.

    peep   mess   tune

    ☐   ☐   ☐

2. He gave the cup a ____.

    tune   kiss   toss

    ☐   ☐   ☐

3. Mom will be mad when she ____ it!

    rule   sees   me

    ☐   ☐   ☐

How to Make Your Little Book

1. Tear.

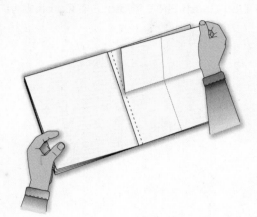

2. Cut.

3. Layer.

4. Fold and staple.

5. Read!

What is the tallest
mountain? Mount Everest!

2

Which country has the most
people? China!

7

What is the longest river?
The Nile!

4

What is our biggest state?
Alaska!

5

What's big in your town?

What's Big on Earth?

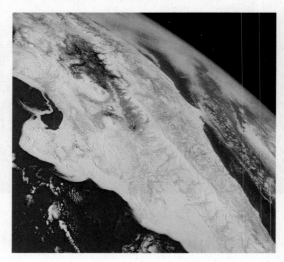

By Kevin Adkins

Which country has the most land? Russia!

What is the deepest ocean? The Pacific!

I turned it up. It let
off fumes. But it did not
make me grow.

2

"You are so big!
It must be all the
spinach."

7

Weeks went by.

4

Months went by.

5

But Carlos and I knew better.

8

The Be-Big Box

Part Two

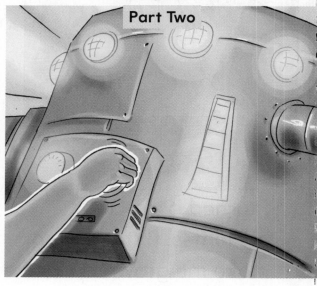

By Beatriz Meléndez
Illustrated by Sebastiá Martí

One day, Mom looked
at me.
"My, my!" Mom said.

6

"Maybe it takes time,"
said Carlos.
"It will happen."

3

In June, I saw an ad for
a Be-Big Box.
I had to have it.

2

It went "huff, huff, huff,
puff." It went "hiss, hiss,
hiss, fizz."

7

"It can make kids grow up.
It will make me so big!"

4

In ten days, it came.
It had huge tubes and pipes
on it.

5

But it did not make me grow.

8

The Be-Big Box

Part One

By Beatriz Meléndez
Illustrated by Sebastiá Martí

I set it up. I turned it on.

6

"What can it do?"asked Carlos.

3

National parks solve
a problem.

2

You can see the glow of a volcano.

7

What can you do in a national
park?

4

You can sit in the shade of a
forest.

5

Which national park
would you like to visit?

8

Our National Parks

By Kevin Adkins

You can climb the rocks
of the desert.

6

They save beautiful places
from being destroyed.

3

2

7

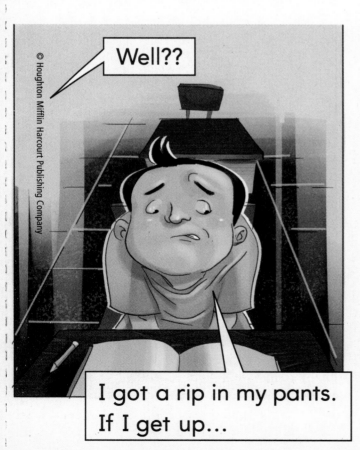

4

5

I can, Pete.
And I will.
Not a peep.

8

Pete Will Not Leave!

Part Two

By Emmet Tubbs
Illustrated by Pam López

I'll go. You can change.

Mrs. Meed?

6

Why not?

3

2

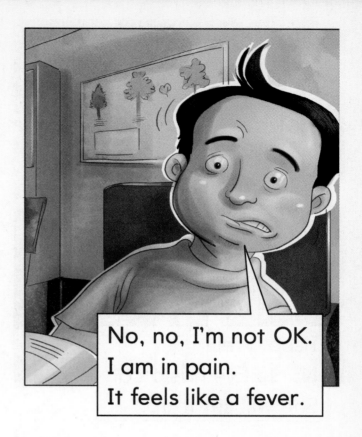

7

4

5

I see. Well!
Nurse Eve has a cot.
She will set it up.

8

49
Pete Will Not Leave!

Part One

By Emmet Tubbs
Illustrated by Pam López

You seem OK to me.

6

Miss Alba, Pete will not leave.

3

Do you ride in a car?
Use a seat belt.

2

In an emergency, call 911.

7

Do you walk to school?
Listen! Look! Be careful!

4

Do you skate?
Wear the right clothes.

5

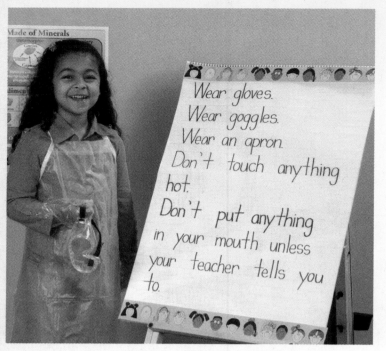

Wear gloves.
Wear goggles.
Wear an apron.
Don't touch anything hot.
Don't put anything in your mouth unless your teacher tells you to.

Be safe! Learn the rules!
Make your own list!

8

Stay Safe

By Kevin Adkins

Do you play at the park?
Don't walk in front of swings!

6

Do you ride a bike?
Wear a helmet.

3

Mike did not eat his yams.
He did not like yams!

2

Mike fed his yams to me!

7

Can I get rid of them?
Then, can go ride my bike.

4

So, bit by bit...

5

OK, Mom.
I am done!

Yams for Lunch

Part Two

By Megan Linke
Illustrated by David Arnau

Bite by bite...

I hate yams.

Mick and Mike sat down.
Lunch time!

2

Mick ate his yams in no time.

7

Yams for Mike.

Yikes!

4

But Mom! I got a lot.
Mick can have mine.

5

Then he ran off to fly his kite.

Yams for Lunch

Part One

By Megan Linke
Illustrated by David Arnau

Eat your yams, Mike.

Fine.

Yams for Mick.

Yes!

Exercise every day.

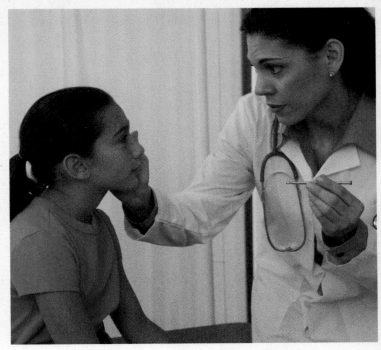

If you are sick, go to the doctor.

2

7

Drink milk.

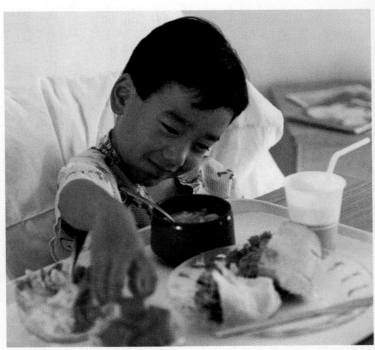

Eat meals that are good for you.

4

5

Get plenty of sleep!
Be healthy! Be happy!

8

Take Care!

By Javier Gutiérrez

Remember!
If you sneeze, use a tissue.

6

Wash fruits and vegetables.

3

Yack yack yack.

If only those kids would quit yelling.

2

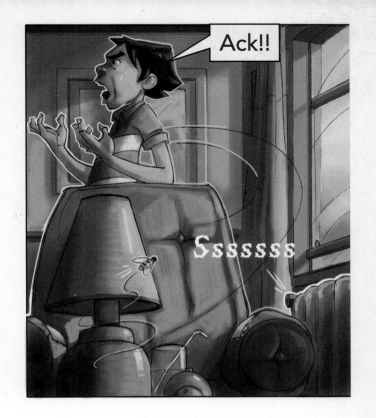

Ack!!

Sssssss

7

At last, it is quiet.

4

Tick tock tick tock tick

5

8

Peace and Quiet

Part Two

By Megan Linke

Illustrated by Sebastiá Martí

6

3

2

7

4

5

Peace and Quiet

Part One

By Megan Linke

Illustrated by Sebastiá Martí

Living things change.
This child will change.

2

The plant grows and gets big.
Do you see the fruit?

7

This kitten is a baby.
She will grow.

4

In time, she will become a cat.

5

Leaves become a plant.

How Things Change

By Candy Rodo

We will plant little seeds.

In time, he will be an adult.

It's time to play!
What games do you like?

Some games are new!
Adults may not know them!

I play some games with friends.

My family likes games.
We play all the time!

It is fun to play games!
Inside or outside!

8

Play Time!

By Alicia Revilla

Some games are very old.
They don't change at all!

6

I play some games by myself.

3

2

7

4

5

It is a nice cave, kids.

8

Jin's Cave

Part Two

By Marvin Hampton
Illustrated by Jordi Redondo

You OK, Mom?

6

Yes! A jet!
Jin is far away!

3

Sun, where is Jin?

2

He sits in his cave.
He wades in the lake.

7

A cave?

Yes! It is by a lake.

4

It is his new home.

5

8

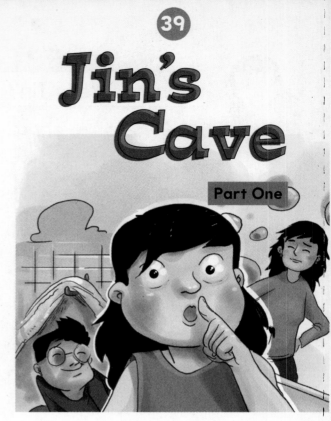

Jin's Cave

Part One

By Marvin Hampton
Illustrated by Jordi Redondo

6

3

This is me!
I was just a baby.

2

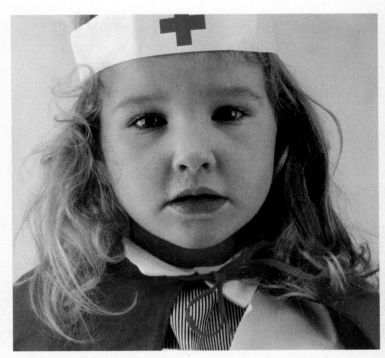

I like space travel!
I want to be an astronaut.

7

I like helping people.
I want to be a doctor!

4

I want to be a doctor, too!
I will work in a hospital.

5

I want to be a gardener!
What will you be?

8

When I Grow Up...

By Luz Acevedo

I like science.
I want to be a scientist!

6

Now I'm older and bigger.
I know what I will be.

3

My birthday is special.
I am older now.

2

Smash! It's broken!
This is fun!

7

At home, I have a party.

4

We hang up a piñata.

5

Birthdays

When is your birthday?
How do you celebrate it?

By Benita Masong

We hit it with a stick.
No peeking!

I bring cupcakes to school.

2

7

4

5

Happy Birthday

Part Two

By Megan Linke

Illustrated by David Arnau

Here is a hose.
Here is a mop. Go!

No.

Nope.

2

7

4

5

Happy Birthday

Part One

By Megan Linke
Illustrated by David Arnau

Where do animals live?
We make homes for some.

2

Look up, in the tree!
See the bird's nest!

7

Some live in burrows.
They are in the ground.

4

Some live in the forest.

5

Some live in a pocket.
A pocket is a cozy home.

8

Where Animals Live

By Candy Rodo

Many live in the desert.

6

Most have a special habitat.

3

Some fish live in oceans.

2

Whales live under the water.
We can see whales, too.

7

Some fish swim with others.

4

This sea turtle swims alone.

5

Mammals swim for a bit.
Then they return to the air.

8

Underwater Animals

By Lionel Charles

A sea lion lives under water.
It is a mammal, not a fish.

6

Some live in ponds or rivers.

3

2

7

4

5

It is called a lake, kid.
You've got a LOT to learn!

8

Gub's New Life
Part Two

By Megan Linke
Illustrated by Sebastiá Martí

A duck?
Hi, Duck!
I am Gub.

6

I am up!

3

Mom, Dad, don't be sad. I must go.

2

I did it!

7

That kid has guts.

4

Can I make it? I can make it!

5

Gub's New Life
Part One

By Megan Linke
Illustrated by Sebastiá Martí

Many animals help us.

Some birds eat mosquitoes.

Bees make honey for us!

Bees also gather pollen.
Pollen helps more plants grow.

All animals are important.

Helpful Animals

By Marc Riba

Some animals have big jobs!

Some keep us company.

All animals eat to live.

2

Some eat grass.

7

Some animals eat fish.

4

Some animals eat nuts.

5

Some animals like treats.
Do you know any who do?

8

What Animals Eat

By Candy Rodo

Some animals eat insects.

6

Some animals eat meat.

3

PLOP!

2

I take it back, Meg. Your cake is not sad.

7

Don't be sad, Mack. It is OK.

4

What can I sell?

5

It is not sad at all.

Bake Sale
Part Two

By Emma Riba
Illustrated by Pam López

We can share.
Let's set up a table together.

That is a sad cake.

2

7

4

5

You bet!
I made a big cake.
It is fit for a king!

8

Bake Sale
Part One

By Emma Riba
Illustrated by Pam López

It is too.
It is sad, sad, sad.

6

I made a cake.
It is for the bake sale.

3

Let's make a journal!
A weather journal!

2

Think about your journal.

7

Look outside.
What is the weather?

4

Is it rainy? Is it sunny?
Is it snowy? Is it windy?

5

Then tell about the weather.
Use your journal!

8

Weather Journal

By María José Fernández

storm

Is it cloudy?
Make a drawing.

6

Today is... Wednesday
April 5, 2006
Temperature 65-73°F

Talk about your plan.
Write the day and date.

3

It is a sunny day.
But is it hot?

2

I will wear a warm coat.
I will wear my gloves and scarf.

7

It is hot!
Let's go outside!

4

Wait for me!
Let's go to the beach!

5

Snowy weather can be fun!

Hot or Cold?

By Candy Rodo

Now it is very cold!
Look at the thermometer!

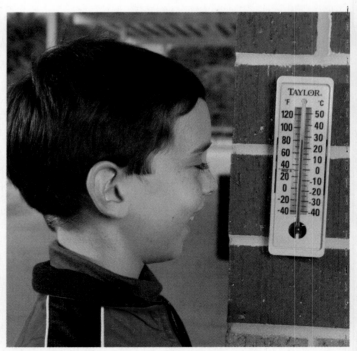

Check the temperature.

I like this cape.
I can tame a wild cat.

2

Nice hat, Cam.

7

Mom and Dad made a plan.

4

Mom hid Cam's cape.
Dad shut the lid.

5

© HMH Supplemental Publishers Inc.

Hat? It is not a hat!
And I am not Cam.
I am Cameron the Great!

8

SUPERCAM
Part Two

By Carla Gacía
Illustrated by David Arnau

The next day, Cam came in.
Cam did not have his cape on.

6

Got him!

3

One day, Cam came in.
He had a cape on.

2

It hit a fan.
The fan hit Dad's hat rack.

7

In this cape, I can fly.
I can fly like a bird!

4

His cape made Mom mad.

5

The hat rack hit Dad.
Dad has had it!

8

SUPERCAM
Part One

By Carla Gacía
Illustrated by David Arnau

His cape made Dad mad, too.

6

Nice cape, Cam.

I am not Cam.
I am Supercam!

3

I look out the window.

2

The rain is going away.
The sky is getting clear.

7

It will be a rainy day!

4

It is raining now!

5

Now we can go outside!

8

Rain

By Candy Rodo

What's that flash?
I see lightning!

6

It is cloudy!

3

Pets need exercise.

2

Give your pets water.

7

Walk your dog in the snow.

4

Dogs need exercise!

5

Take care of your pets!
Play with them everyday!

Pets and the Weather

By Sebastian Vila

Is it really hot?
Don't wait!

Walk your dog in the rain.

2

7

4

5

And just in time for dinner.

8

Mack the Wild Poodle
Part Two

By Megan Linke

Illustrated by Maria Morell

0

Mack! Mack!

6

Ack! It bit me!

3

I did it! I am free.

8

Mack the Wild Poodle
Part One

By Megan Linke
Illustrated by Maria Morell

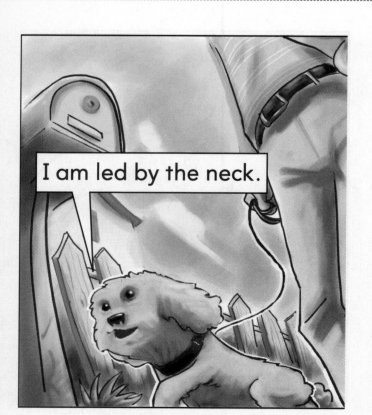

I am led by the neck.

6

As a pet, I sit.
I sit on a mat all day.

3

Follow the sign!
See the police station.

2

You can help, too!
Help your town. Recycle!

7

The fire alarm rings!
Trucks leave the fire station!

4

They don't need a map!
They locate the building!

5

Help new students.
Show them they belong!

8

Helping in the Neighborhood

By Gladys Lalane

Read the news.
Learn what you can do.

6

The police keep us safe.
They help us.

3

2

7

4

5

A sick kid gets hot soup!

Rick's Trick

By Megan Linke
Illustrated by Pam López

Not Bad.

I can't, Dad.
I am sick.

We walk in the library.
Let's look for a book.

2

See the bicycle wheels?
They go round and round.

7

Do we need to go far?
We can ride in a car!

4

A train goes past!
It zooms so fast!

5

On the Move!

By Candy Rodo

This is our neighborhood!
It is on the move!

8

A worker climbs up.
Then he climbs down.

6

We play ball at the park.
Let's race to home base.

3

Pat had a hat.
It did not sit still.

2

Pip the cat ran off.

7

It ran.
It hit a wall.

4

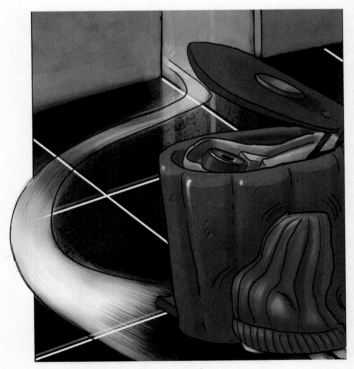

It ran behind a bin.
It hid.

5

At last, Pat got his hat on.

SIT STILL Hat!

By Megan Linke
Illustrated by Pam López

Pip!

Pat picked it up.

It fell off a table.

See the cat and dog?
Do they get along?

2

Some do.

7

See the chicken and cat?
Do they get along?

4

Some do.

5

Think about animals you know.
Do they get along?

Animals in My Neighborhood

By Lorenzo Adama

See the cat and fish?
Do they get along?

Some do.

2

7

4

5

I Am No Rat!

By Camilia Yuen
Illustrated by Pam López

Our town has a camp.
It is a lot of fun!

2

Then, we go back home!

7

Neighbors play tag.

4

Pals play games.

5

Back to our neighborhood!

Going to Camp!

By Galila Ali

We hike in the woods.

We stay in tents!
There are no buildings!

2

7

4

5

8

11

Packing for Camp

By Megan Linke
Illustrated by David Arnau

6

3

This family is big.

2

See the dad and his kids?
This family is special.

7

This family has fun.

4

How can we tell?

5

Families care. Families listen.
Tell about your family.

8

All Families Are Special!

By Leslie Wong

See the mom and her girl?
This family is special.

6

This family is small.

3

2

7

4

5

Are You Mad, Dad?

By Emma Riba

Illustrated by Sebastiá Martí

Take a walk.

2

Hear the sounds.

7

Smell the flowers.

4

See his face!

5

Share a picnic!
How does it taste?

A Walk in the Park

By Marcos Granados

Touch the grass.

Use the five senses.

Mom got Nat.
Tag! Nat is it.

2

I am not playing.

7

Bob got Gab.
Tag! Gab is it.

4

Gab got me.

5

I am not a fan of tag.

Tag

By Roberto Gómez
Illustrated by Jordi Redondo

Sob! I am not it.

Nat got Bob.
Tag! Bob is it.

We can make cookies!
What is your favorite Kind?

2

Hot! Do not touch!

7

Add chips.

4

Mix it up!

5

Ready!
Can you smell them?

8

What's Cooking?

By Lucía Casanovas

Can you count them?

6

milk

eggs

flour

sugar

See what we need?

3

2

7

4

5

8

Nan's Mistake

By Cristina Moreno
Illustrated by Maria Morell

6

3

We like baseball!

We smell the popcorn!
Mmmmm!

We touch them.

He is out!

We win!
Can you hear us?

Baseball!

By Candy Rodo

We taste the hotdog.
Yummy!

We see the players.

Sam sat and sat.

Sam!
Grab a bat.

Sam's Big Day

By Sofia Lee
Illustrated by Pam López

Sam stood at bat.

Sam sat.

We have a great teacher!

2

We learn about shapes.

7

We share.

4

We add.

5

We love our class!

Our School

By Luc Alexandre

We ask questions.

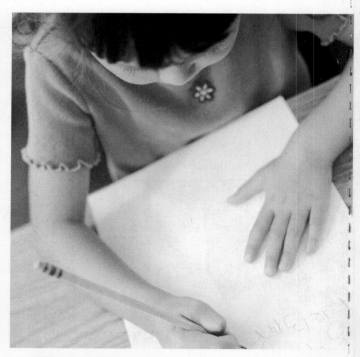

We write.

Are you ready?

2

Do you see the white clouds?

7

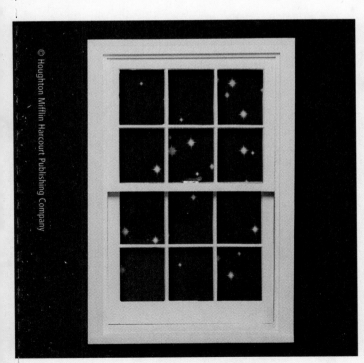

Look out the window.
What do you see?

4

Do you see the Moon?

5

Do you see the big yellow Sun?

Blue Sky

By Candy Rodo

Do you see the blue sky?

Let's learn about the sky!